FREMDSPRACHENTEXTE

James Thurber

Stories and Fables for Our Time

Mit Zeichnungen
des Verfassers

Herausgegeben
von Harald Beck

Nachwort
von Werner Gotzmann

Philipp Reclam jun. Stuttgart

Diese Ausgabe darf nur in der Bundesrepublik Deutschland, in Österreich und in der Schweiz vertrieben werden.

RECLAMS UNIVERSAL-BIBLIOTHEK Nr. 9232

Durchgesehene und bibliographisch ergänzte Ausgabe 2004
Gesamtherstellung: Reclam, Ditzingen. Printed in Germany 2004
RECLAM, UNIVERSAL-BIBLIOTHEK und
RECLAMS UNIVERSAL-BIBLIOTHEK sind eingetragene Marken der Philipp Reclam jun. GmbH & Co., Stuttgart
ISBN 3-15-009232-9

www.reclam.de

The Human Being and the Dinosaur

Ages ago in a wasteland of time and a wilderness of space, Man, in upper case, and dinosaur, in lower, first came face to face. They stood like stones for a long while, wary and watchful, taking each other in. Something told the dinosaur that he beheld before him the coming glory and terror of the world, and in the still air of the young planet he seemed to catch the faint smell of his own inevitable doom.

"Greetings, stupid," said Man. "Behold in me the artfully articulated architect of the future, the chosen species, the certain survivor, the indestructible one, the monarch of all you survey, and of all that everyone else surveys, for that matter. On the other hand, you are, curiously enough, for all your size, a member of the inconsequent ephemera. You are one of God's moder-

2 **wasteland:** Ödland, Wüste.
3 **upper case:** Großbuchstaben.
lower (*case*): Kleinbuchstaben.
5 **wary:** vorsichtig, bedachtsam.
watchful: wachsam, gespannt.
to take s.o. in: jdn. von oben bis unten betrachten, mustern.
6 **to behold:** erblicken.
9 **inevitable:** unausweichlich.
doom: Untergang, Verderben.
10f. **artfully** (adv.): 1. schlau, listig; 2. kunstvoll.
11 **articulated:** 1. artikuliert, fähig zu sprechen; 2. gegliedert (auf den Körperbau bezogen).
12 **indestructable:** unzerstörbar.
16 **inconsequent:** belanglos, irrelevant.
ephemera: Eintagsfliege, vorübergehende Erscheinung.

ately amusing early experiments, a frail footnote to natural history, a contraption in a museum for future Man to marvel at, an excellent example of Jehovah's jejune juvenilia."

The dinosaur sighed with a sound like thunder.

"Perpetuating your species," Man continued, "would be foolish and futile."

"The missing link is not lost," said the dinosaur sorrowfully. "It's hiding."

Man paid the doomed dinosaur no mind. "If there were no Man it would be necessary to create one," said Man, "for God moves in mysterious, but inefficient, ways, and He needs help. Man will go on forever, but you will be one with the mammoth and the mastodon, for monstrosity is the behemother of extinction."

1 **frail:** schwach, zerbrechlich, vergänglich.
2 **contraption** (coll.): Apparat, verrücktes Ding.
3 **to marvel at s.th.:** etwas bestaunen.
4 **jejune:** (fig.) mager, fade.
juvenilia: Jugendwerke.
6 **to perpetuate:** erhalten, fortbestehen lassen.
7 **futile:** überflüssig, nutzlos.
8 **missing link:** Gemeint ist in Anlehnung an Darwin das fehlende Glied in der Kette zwischen Affe und Mensch.
8f. **sorrowfully** (adv.): unglücklich, bekümmert.
10 **to pay no mind** (dial.): keine Aufmerksamkeit schenken.
doomed: verloren, dem Untergang geweiht.
14 **mammoth:** Mammut.
mastodon: Mastodon (ausgestorbene Elefantenart, zur Mammutfamilie gehörig).
14f. **monstrosity:** Monstrosität, Widernatürlichkeit.
15 **behemother:** Wortspiel mit *behemoth* ›biblisches Untier‹ und *mother*; zugrunde liegt das Sprichwort »Necessity is the mother of invention« (»Not macht erfinderisch«).
extinction: Vernichtung, Ausrottung.

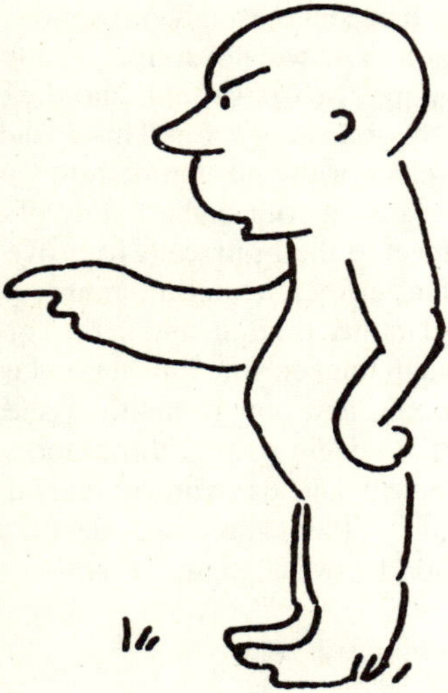

“There are worse things than being extinct,” said the dinosaur sourly, “and one of them is being you.”

Man strutted a little pace and flexed his muscles. “You cannot even commit murder,” he said, “for murder requires a mind. You are capable only of dinosaurslaughter. You and your ilk are incapable of devising increasingly effective methods of destroying your own species

1 **extinct:** ausgerottet, ausgelöscht.
2 **sourly** (adv.): mürrisch, bitter.
3 **to strut:** (herum)stolzieren.
to flex one’s muscles: seine Muskeln spielen lassen.
5 f. **dinosaurslaughter:** Wortschöpfung zu *manslaughter* ›Totschlag‹.
6 **ilk:** Familie, Art, Gattung.
to devise: erdenken, ersinnen, erfinden.

and, at the same time, increasingly miraculous methods of keeping it extant. You will never live to know the two-party system, the multi-party system, and the one-party system. You will be gone long before I have made this the best of all possible worlds, no matter how possible all other worlds may be. In your highest state of evolution you could not develop the brain cells to prove innocent men guilty, even after their acquittal. You are all wrong in the crotch, and in the cranium, and in the cortex. But I have wasted enough time on you. I must use these fingers which God gave me, and now probably wishes He had kept for Himself, to begin writing those noble volumes about Me which will one day run to several hundred billion items, many of them about war, death, conquest, decline, fall, blood, sweat, tears, threats, warnings,

1 **miraculous:** wunderbar, erstaunlich.
2 **extant:** existierend, erhalten.
3 **multi-party system:** Vielparteiensystem.
4f. **the best of all possible worlds:** die beste aller möglichen Welten; Formel des deutschen Philosophen Gottfried Wilhelm Leibniz (1646–1716).
8 **acquittal:** Freispruch.
9 **crotch:** Schritt, Genitalien.
cranium: Schädel.
cortex: Hirnrinde.
14 **billion:** Milliarde (AE).
item: Artikel, Eintrag.
conquest: Eroberung.
15 **decline / fall:** Anspielung auf das Werk *The History of the Decline and Fall of the Roman Empire* (6 Bde., 1776–88; dt. *Geschichte des Verfalls und Untergangs des Römischen Reiches*, 1779–1806) des englischen Historikers und Schriftstellers Edward Gibbon (1737–94).
blood / sweat / tears: Anspielung auf Churchills berühmtes Wort aus seiner Unterhausrede vom Mai 1940: »I have nothing to offer but blood, toil, tears and sweat« (»Ich habe nichts zu bieten als Blut, Mühsal, Tränen und Schweiß«).

boasts, hopelessness, hell, heels, and whores. There will be little enough about you and your ilk and your kith and your kin, for after all, who were you and your ilk and your kith and your kin? Good day and goodbye," said Man in conclusion. "I shall see to it that your species receives a decent burial, with some simple ceremony."

Man, as it turned out, was right. The dinosaur and his ilk and his kith and his kin died not long after, still in lower case, but with a curious smile of satisfaction, or something of the sort, on their ephemeral faces.

MORAL: *The noblest study of mankind is Man, says Man.*

1 **boast:** Prahlerei.
heel (slang): gemeiner Kerl, Schuft.
whore: Hure.
2f. **kith and kin:** Bekanntschaft und Verwandtschaft.
6 **decent:** anständig.
10 **ephemeral:** vergänglich, flüchtig.
11 **The noblest study of mankind is Man:** Anspielung auf ein geflügeltes Wort, das der englische Dichter Alexander Pope (1688–1744) in seinem *Essay on Man* II,1 geprägt hat: »The proper study of Mankind is Man.«

The Remarkable Case of Mr Bruhl

Samuel O. Bruhl was just an ordinary-looking citizen, like you and me, except for a curious, shoe-shaped scar on his left cheek, which he got when he fell against a wagon-tongue in his youth. He had a good job as treasurer for a syrup-and-fondant concern, a large, devout wife, two tractable daughters, and a nice home in Brooklyn. He worked from nine to five, took in a show occasionally, played a bad, complacent game of golf, and was usually in bed by eleven o'clock. The Bruhls had a dog named Bert, a small circle of friends, and an old sedan. They had made a comfortable, if unexciting, adjustment to life.

There was no reason in the world why Samuel Bruhl shouldn't have lived along quietly until he died of some commonplace malady. He was a man designed by Nature for an uneventful life, an inexpensive but respectable

3 **scar:** Narbe, Mal.
5 **wagon-tongue:** Wagendeichsel.
5f. **treasurer:** Schatzmeister, Kassierer.
6 **syrup-and-fondant concern:** Sirup-und-Fondant-Unternehmen.
devout: ergeben, zugetan.
7 **tractable:** folgsam, umgänglich.
8 **to take in:** hier: besuchen.
9 **complacent:** selbstzufrieden.
11 **sedan** (AE): Limousine.
12 **to make an adjustment:** sich anpassen.
unexciting: ereignislos, ruhig.
16 **commonplace:** alltäglich, gewöhnlich.
malady: Krankheit, Leiden.
17 **uneventful:** ereignislos.
inexpensive: preiswert.

funeral, and a modest stone marker. All this you would have predicted had you observed his colourless comings and goings, his mild manner, the small stature of his dreams. He was, in brief, the sort of average citizen that observers of Judd Gray thought Judd Gray was. And precisely as that mild little family man was abruptly hurled into an incongruous tragedy, so was Samuel Bruhl suddenly picked out of the hundreds of men just like him and marked for an extravagant and unpredictable end. Oddly enough it was the shoe-shaped scar on his left cheek which brought to his heels a Nemesis he had never dreamed of. A blemish on his heart, a tic in his soul would have been different; one would have blamed Bruhl for whatever anguish an emotional or spiritual flaw laid him open to, but it is ironical indeed when the Furies

1 **stone marker:** Gedenkstein.
2 **to predict:** vorhersagen, prophezeien.
3 **stature:** Größe, Format.
5 **Gray:** Judd G., »a very ordinary married man«, wurde im Januar 1928 zusammen mit seiner Komplizin wegen Mordes an ihrem Ehemann, Albert Snyder, hingerichtet.
7 **to hurl:** schleudern, stürzen.
incongruous: unangemessen.
9 **to mark:** bestimmen, auserwählen.
extravagant: übertrieben, überspannt.
unpredictable: unvorhersagbar.
11 **to bring s.th. to s.o.'s heels:** jdm. etwas an die Fersen heften.
Nemesis: Nemesis, griechische Rachegöttin; (fig.) strafende Gerechtigkeit.
12 **blemish:** Makel.
tic: Zucken.
14 **anguish:** Qual, Pein.
flaw: Fehler, Makel.
15 **to lay s.o. open to s.th.:** jdn. einer Sache aussetzen.
Fury: Furie (Rachegöttin der römischen Mythologie).

ride down a man who has been guilty of nothing worse than an accident in his childhood.

Samuel O. Bruhl looked very much like George ("Shoescar") Clinigan. Clinigan had that same singular shoe-shaped scar on his left cheek. There was also a general resemblance in height, weight, and complexion. A careful study would have revealed very soon that Clinigan's eyes were shifty and Bruhl's eyes were clear, and that the syrup-and-fondant company's treasurer had a more pleasant mouth and a higher forehead than the gangster and racketeer, but at a glance the similarity was remarkable.

Had Clinigan not become notorious, this prank of Nature would never have been detected, but Clinigan did become notorious and dozens of persons observed that he looked like Bruhl. They saw Clinigan's picture in the papers the day he was shot, and the day after, and the day after that. Presently someone in the syrup-and-fondant concern mentioned to someone else that Clinigan looked like Mr Bruhl, remarkably like Mr Bruhl. Soon everybody in the place had commented on it, among themselves, and to Mr Bruhl.

Mr Bruhl rather laughed it off at first, but one day when Clinigan had been in the hospital a week, a cop peered

6 **resemblance:** Ähnlichkeit.
complexion: Aussehen.
8 **shifty:** unstet, verschlagen.
11 **racketeer:** Gangster, Ganove.
13 **notorious:** allbekannt, berüchtigt.
prank: Streich, Kapriole.
18 **presently** (adv.): bald darauf.
23 **to laugh s.th. off:** sich lachend über etwas hinwegsetzen.
24 **cop** (slang): Polizist, ‚Bulle'.
to peer: in Augenschein nehmen, fixieren.

closely at Mr Bruhl when he was on his way home from work. After that, the little treasurer noticed a number of other strangers staring at him with mingled surprise and alarm. One small, dark man hastily thrust a hand into his coat pocket and paled slightly.

Mr Bruhl began to worry. He began to imagine things. "I hope this fellow Clinigan doesn't pull through," he said one morning at breakfast. "He's a bad actor. He's better off dead."

"Oh, he'll pull through," said Mrs Bruhl, who had been reading the morning paper. "It says here he'll pull through. But it says they'll shoot him again. It says they're sure to shoot him again."

The morning after the night that Clinigan left the hospital, secretly, by a side door, and disappeared into the town, Bruhl decided not to go to work. "I don't feel so good today," he said to his wife. "Would you call up the office and tell them I'm sick?"

"You don't look well," said his wife. "You really don't look well. Get down, Bert," she added, for the dog had jumped upon her lap and whined. The animal knew that something was wrong.

That evening Bruhl, who had mooned about the house all day, read in the papers that Clinigan had vanished, but was believed to be somewhere in the city. His various rackets required his presence, at least until he made

4 **to thrust:** schieben, stecken.
5 **to pale:** blaß werden.
7 **to pull through:** durchkommen.
8 **bad actor:** übler Kunde.
21 **to whine:** winseln, jaulen.
23 **to moon:** herumwandern.
26 **racket:** Machenschaft, Gaunerei.

enough money to skip out with; he had left the hospital penniless. Rival gangsters, the papers said, were sure to seek him out, to hunt him down, to give it to him again. "Give him what again?" asked Mrs Bruhl when she read this. "Let's talk about something else," said her husband.

It was little Joey, the office-boy at the syrup-and-fondant company, who first discovered that Mr Bruhl was afraid. Joey, who went about with tennis shoes on, entered the treasurer's office suddenly – flung open the door and started to say something. "Good God!" cried Mr Bruhl, rising from his chair. "Why, what's the matter, Mr Bruhl?" asked Joey. Other little things happened. The switchboard girl phoned Mr Bruhl's desk one afternoon and said there was a man waiting to see him, a Mr Globe. "What's he look like?" asked Bruhl, who didn't know anybody named Globe. "He's small and dark," said the girl. "A small, dark man?" said Bruhl. "Tell him I'm out. Tell him I've gone to California." The personnel, comparing notes, decided at length that the treasurer was afraid of being mistaken for Shoescar and put on the spot. They said nothing to Mr Bruhl about this, because they were forbidden to by Ollie Breithofter, a fattish

1 **to skip** (slang): abhauen, verduften.
3 **to hunt s.o. down:** jdn. zur Strecke bringen.
to give it to s.o.: es jdm. geben, heimzahlen.
14 **switchboard girl:** Telephonistin.
19 **personnel:** Personal, Belegschaft.
19f. **to compare notes:** sich beraten, beratschlagen.
21f. **to put s.o. on the spot** (slang): jdn. aufs Korn nehmen.
23 **fattish:** dicklich.

clerk who was a tireless and inventive practical joker and who had an idea.

As the hunt went on for Clinigan and he still wasn't found and killed, Mr Bruhl lost weight and grew extremely fidgety. He began to figure out new ways of getting to work, one requiring the use of two different ferry lines; he ate his lunch in, he wouldn't answer bells, he cried out when anyone dropped anything, and he ran into stores or banks when cruising taxidrivers shouted at him. One morning, in setting the house to rights, Mrs Bruhl found

1 **tireless:** unermüdlich.
inventive: erfinderisch, einfallsreich.
practical joker: jd., der anderen gern einen Streich spielt.
5 **fidgety:** unruhig, zappelig.
9 **to cruise:** kreuzen.
10 **to set s.th. to rights:** etwas in Ordnung bringen, aufräumen.

a revolver under his pillow. "I found a revolver under your pillow," she told him that night. "Burglars are bad in this neighbourhood," he said. "You oughtn't to have a revolver," she said. They argued about it, he irritably, she uneasily, until time for bed. As Bruhl was undressing, after locking and bolting all the doors, the telephone rang. "It's for you, Sam," said Mrs Bruhl. Her husband went slowly to the phone, passing Bert on the way. "I wish I was you," he said to the dog, and took up the receiver. "Get this, Shoescar," said a husky voice. "We trailed you where you are, see? You're cooked." The receiver at the other end was hung up. Bruhl shouted. His wife came running. "What is it, Sam, what is it?" she cried. Bruhl, pale, sick-looking, had fallen into a chair. "They got me," he moaned. "They got me." Slowly, deviously, Minnie Bruhl got it out of her husband that he had been mistaken for Clinigan and that he was cooked. Mrs Bruhl was not very quick mentally, but she had a certain intuition and this intuition told her, as she trembled there in her nightgown above her broken husband, that this was the work of Ollie Breithofter. She instantly phoned Ollie Breithofter's wife and, before she hung up, had got the truth out of Mrs Breithofter. It was Ollie who had called.

2 **burglar:** Einbrecher.
4 **irritably** (adv.): gereizt, nervös.
6 **to bolt:** verriegeln.
10 **husky:** heiser, rauh.
11 **to trail:** aufspüren.
cooked (slang): geliefert, erledigt.
15 **to moan:** stöhnen, ächzen.
16 **deviously** (adv.): auf Umwegen.
20 **nightgown:** Nachthemd.
broken: (fig.) gebrochen, am Boden zerstört.

The treasurer of the Maskonsett Syrup & Fondant Company, Inc., was so relieved to know that the gangs weren't after him that he admitted frankly at the office next day that Ollie had fooled him for a minute. Mr Bruhl even joined in the laughter and wisecracking, which went on all day. After that, for almost a week, the mild little man had comparative peace of mind. The papers said very little about Clinigan now. He had completely disappeared. Gang warfare had died down for the time being.

One Sunday morning Mr Bruhl went for an automobile ride with his wife and daughters. They had driven about a mile through Brooklyn streets when, glancing in the mirror above his head, Mr Bruhl observed a blue sedan just behind him. He turned off into the next side street, and the sedan turned off too. Bruhl made another turn, and the sedan followed him. "Where are you going, dear?" asked Mrs Bruhl. Mr Bruhl didn't answer her, he speeded up, he drove terrifically fast, he turned corners so wildly that the rear wheels swung around. A traffic cop shrilled at him. The younger daughter screamed. Bruhl drove right on, weaving in and out. Mrs Bruhl began to berate him wildly. "Have you lost your mind, Sam?" she shouted. Mr Bruhl looked behind him. The sedan was no

2 **Inc.:** Abk. für *Incorporated* (*Company*): eingetragen(e Firma) (Kapitalgesellschaft in den USA; entspricht der Aktiengesellschaft).
4 **to fool s.o.:** jdn. zum Narren halten, hinters Licht führen.
5 **wisecracking:** Witzeleien.
7 **comparative:** verhältnismäßig.
9 **gang warfare:** Bandenkrieg.
22 **to weave:** hier: sich (durch)schlängeln.
23 **to berate:** heftig schimpfen, zanken.

longer to be seen. He slowed up. "Let's go home," he said. "I've had enough of this."

A month went by without incident (thanks largely to Mrs Breithofter) and Samuel Bruhl began to be himself again. On the day that he was practically normal once more, Sluggy Pensiotta, alias Killer Lewis, alias Stranger Koetschke, was shot. Sluggy was the leader of the gang that had sworn to get Shoescar Clinigan. The papers instantly took up the gang-war story where they had left off. Pictures of Clinigan were published again. The slaying of Pensiotta, said the papers, meant but one thing: it meant that Shoescar Clinigan was cooked. Mr Bruhl, reading this, went gradually to pieces once more.

After another week of skulking about, starting at every noise, and once almost fainting when an automobile backfired near him, Samuel Bruhl began to take on a remarkable new appearance. He talked out of the corner of his mouth, his eyes grew shifty. He looked more and more like Shoescar Clinigan. He snarled at his wife. Once he called her "Babe," and he had never called her anything but Minnie. He kissed her in a strange, new way, acting rough, almost brutal. At the office he was mean and overbearing. He used peculiar language. One night when the Bruhls had friends in for bridge – old Mr Creegan and his wife – Bruhl suddenly appeared from

6 **sluggy:** träge, langsam.
10 f. **to slay:** töten, morden.
14 **to skulk:** sich verstecken, drücken; schleichen.
16 **to backfire:** eine Fehlzündung haben.
19 **to snarl:** knurren, fauchen.
20 **babe** (slang): ‚Puppe'.
23 **overbearing:** arrogant, anmaßend.
peculiar: eigenartig, seltsam.

upstairs with a pair of scarlet pyjamas on, smoking a cigarette, and gripping his revolver. After a few loud and incoherent remarks of a boastful nature, he let fly at a clock on the mantel, and hit it squarely in the middle. Mrs Bruhl screamed. Mr Creegan fainted. Bert, who was in the kitchen, howled. "What's the matta you?" snarled Bruhl. "Ya bunch of softies."

Quite by accident, Mrs Bruhl discovered, hidden away in a closet, eight or ten books on gangs and gangsters, which Bruhl had put there. They included "Al Capone," "You Can't Win," "10,000 Public Enemies" and a lot of others; and they were all well thumbed. Mrs Bruhl realized that it was high time something was done, and she determined to have a doctor for her husband. For two or three days Bruhl had not gone to work. He lay around in his bedroom, in his red pyjamas, smoking cigarettes. The office phoned once or twice. When Mrs Bruhl urged him to get up and dress and go to work, he laughed and patted her roughly on the head. "It's a knockover, kid," he said. "We'll be sitting pretty. To hell with it."

1 **scarlet:** scharlachrot.
3 **incoherent:** unzusammenhängend.
boastful: prahlerisch, überheblich.
to let fly: schießen.
4 **mantel:** Kurzform von *mantelpiece:* Kaminsims.
squarely (adv.): direkt.
6 **matta:** matter.
7 **ya:** *you.*
softy (slang): Waschlappen, Schwächling.
9 **closet:** Wandschrank.
12 **well thumbed:** abgegriffen.
18 **to pat:** tätscheln, klopfen.
19 **knockover** (slang): hier: Kinderspiel, ‚kleine Fische'.
20 **to be sitting pretty** (slang): in Sicherheit sein.

The doctor who finally came and slipped into Bruhl's bedroom was very grave when he emerged. "This is a psychosis," he said, "a definite psychosis. Your husband is living in a world of fantasy. He has built up a curious defence mechanism against something or other." The doctor suggested that a psychiatrist be called in, but after he had gone Mrs Bruhl decided to take her husband out of town on a trip. The Maskonsett Syrup & Fondant Company, Inc., was very fine about it. Mr Scully said of course. "Sam is very valuable to us, Mrs Bruhl," said Mr Scully, "and we all hope he'll be all right." Just the same he had Mr Bruhl's accounts examined, when Mrs Bruhl had gone.

Oddly enough, Samuel Bruhl was amenable to the idea of going away. "I need a rest," he said. "You're right. Let's get the hell out of here." He seemed normal up to the time they set out for the Grand Central and then he insisted on leaving from the 125th Street station. Mrs Bruhl took exception to this, as being ridiculous, whereupon her doting husband snarled at her. "God, what a dumb moll *I* picked," he said to Minnie Bruhl, and he added bitterly that if the heat was put to him it would be his own babe who was to blame. "And what do you think of *that*?" he said, pushing her to the floor of the cab.

3 **psychosis:** Psychose (Geisteskrankheit).
12 **accounts:** Abrechnungen, Bücher.
14 **amenable:** zugänglich.
19 **to take exception to s.th.:** gegen etwas Einwendungen machen, an etwas Anstoß nehmen.
20 **doting:** vernarrt (in jdn.); kindisch, senil.
21 **moll** (slang): Gangsterbraut.
22 **to put the heat on s.o.** (slang): jdn. unter Druck setzen.

They went to a little inn in the mountains. It wasn't a very nice place, but the rooms were clean and the meals were good. There was no form of entertainment, except a Tom Thumb golf course and an uneven tennis court, but Mr Bruhl didn't mind. He said it was too cold outdoors, anyway. He stayed indoors, reading and smoking. In the evening he played the mechanical piano in the dining-room. He liked to play "More Than You Know" over and over again. One night, about nine o'clock, he was putting in his seventh or eighth nickel when four men walked into the dining-room. They were silent men, wearing overcoats, and carrying what appeared to be cases for musical instruments. They took out various kinds of guns from their cases, quickly, expertly, and walked over toward Bruhl, keeping step. He turned just in time to see them line up four abreast and aim at him. Nobody else was in the room. There was a cumulative roar and a series of flashes. Mr Bruhl fell and the men walked out in single file, rapidly, nobody having said a word.

Mrs Bruhl, state police, and the hotel manager tried to get the wounded man to talk. Chief Witznitz of the nearest town's police force tried it. It was no good. Bruhl only

3 f. **Tom Thumb golf course:** Minigolfplatz (*Tom Thumb:* (Däumling).
4 **uneven:** uneben, holprig.
8 **»More Than You Know«:** Lied von Vincent Youmans, Billy Rose und Edward Eliscu (1919).
10 **nickel:** Fünfcentstück.
15 **to keep step:** Schritt halten.
16 **to line up:** (sich) aufreihen.
abreast: nebeneinander.
17 **cumulative:** anschwellend.
18 **roar:** Krachen, Donner.
19 **single file:** Gänsemarsch.

snarled and told them to go away and let him alone. Finally, Commissioner O'Donnell of the New York City Police Department arrived at the hospital. He asked Bruhl what the men looked like. "I don't know what they looked like," snarled Bruhl, "and if I did know I wouldn't tell you." He was silent a moment, then: "Cop!" he added, bitterly. The Commissioner sighed and turned away. "They're all like that," he said to the others in the room. "They never talk." Hearing this, Mr Bruhl smiled, a pleased smile, and closed his eyes.

The Trial of the Old Watchdog

An old experienced collie, who had been a faithful country watchdog for many years, was arrested one summer's day and accused of the first-degree murder of a lamb. Actually, the lamb had been slain by a notorious red fox who had planted the still-warm body of his victim in the collie's kennel.

The trial was held in a kangaroo court presided over by Judge Wallaby. The jury consisted of foxes, and

2 **Commissioner:** Kommissar.
14 **first-degree murder** (AE): Mord ersten Grades.
15 **to slay:** töten, erlegen.
notorious: berüchtigt.
16 **to plant:** einschmuggeln, plazieren.
17 **kennel:** Hundehütte.
18 **kangaroo court** (coll.): inoffizieller Gerichtshof.
to preside over: den Vorsitz führen.
19 **wallaby:** kleines Känguru.

all the spectators were foxes. A fox named Reynard was prosecuting attorney. "Morning, Judge," he said.

"God bless you, boy, and good luck," replied Judge Wallaby jovially.

A poodle named Beau, an old friend and neighbour of the collie, represented the accused watchdog. "Good morning, Judge," said the poodle.

"Now I don't want you to be too clever," the Judge warned him. "Cleverness should be confined to the weaker side. That's only fair."

A blind woodchuck was the first creature to take the stand, and she testified that she saw the collie kill the lamb.

"The witness is blind!" protested the poodle.

"No personalities, please," said the Judge severely. "Perhaps the witness saw the murder in a dream or a vision. This would give her testimony the authority of revelation."

"I wish to call a character witness," said the poodle.

1 **Reynard:** Reinecke.
2 **prosecuting attorney:** Staatsanwalt, Vertreter der Anklage.
5 **jovially** (adv.): heiter, lustig.
6 **poodle:** Pudel.
Beau: sprechender Name (von frz. *beau* ›schön‹).
10 **confined:** begrenzt, beschränkt.
12 **woodchuck:** Waldmurmeltier.
12f. **to take the stand:** in den Zeugenstand treten, als Zeuge aussagen.
13 **to testify:** bezeugen.
16 **personalities:** Anzüglichkeiten, persönliche Bemerkungen.
18 **testimony:** Zeugnis, Aussage.
19 **revelation:** Offenbarung.
20 **character witness:** Leumundszeuge.

"We have no character witnesses," said Reynard smoothly, "but we have some charming character assassins."

One of these, a fox named Burrows, was called to the stand. "I didn't actually see this lamb killer kill this lamb," said Burrows, "but I almost did."

"That's close enough," said Judge Wallaby.

"Objection," barked the poodle.

"Objection overruled," said the Judge. "It's getting late. Has the jury reached a verdict?"

The forefox of the jury stood up. "We find the defendant guilty," he said, "but we think it would be better to acquit him, nonetheless. If we hang the defendant, his punishment will be over. But if we acquit him of such dark crimes as murder, concealing the body, and associating with poodles and defence attorneys, nobody will ever trust him again, and he will be suspect all the days of his life. Hanging is too good for him, and much too quick."

"Guilt by exoneration!" Reynard cried. "What a lovely way to end his usefulness!"

2f. **assassin:** (gedungener) Mörder.
4 **Burrows:** sprechender Name (von *to burrow* ›wühlen, graben‹).
8 **objection:** Einspruch.
9 **to overrule:** hier (jur.): (einen Einspruch) abweisen, ablehnen.
10 **verdict:** Urteil.
11 **forefox:** Wortschöpfung zu *foreman* ›Sprecher der Geschworenen‹.
defendant: Angeklagter.
12 **to acquit:** freisprechen.
13 **nonetheless:** trotzdem.
17 **suspect:** verdächtig.
20 **exoneration:** Entlastung, Freispruch.

And so the case was dismissed and court was adjourned, and everybody went home to tell about it.

MORAL: *Thou shalt not blindfold justice by pulling the wool over her eyes.*

The Lover and His Lass

An arrogant grey parrot and his arrogant mate listened, one African afternoon, in disdain and derision, to the lovemaking of a lover and his lass, who happened to be hippopotamuses.

"He calls her Snooky-Ookums," said Mrs Grey. "Can you believe that?"

"No," said Grey. "I don't see how any male in his right mind could entertain affection for a female that has no more charm than a capsized bathtub."

1 **to dismiss a case:** einen Fall, eine Verhandlung abschließen.
to adjourn: schließen, vertagen.
3 **thou shalt not** (arch.): *you shall not.*
to blindfold: die Augen verbinden.
3 f. **to pull the wool over s.o.'s eyes** (fig.): jdn. hinters Licht führen.
5 **the lover and his lass:** Anspielung auf ein Lied aus Shakespeares *As You Like It* V,3: »It was a lover and his lass« (*lass:* Mädchen).
6 **mate:** Gefährtin, Gemahlin.
7 **disdain:** Verachtung, Geringschätzung.
derision: Hohn, Spott.
9 **hippopotamus:** Nilpferd.
10 **Snooky-Ookums:** erfundener Kosename; etwa: Schnuckelchen. Lied von Irving Berlin (1913).
13 **to entertain affection:** Zuneigung hegen.
14 **to capsize:** kentern, umstürzen.

"Capsized bathtub, indeed!" exclaimed Mrs Grey. "Both of them have the appeal of a coastwise fruit steamer with a cargo of waterlogged basketballs."

But it was spring, and the lover and his lass were young, and they were oblivious of the scornful comments of their sharp-tongued neighbours, and they continued to bump each other around in the water, happily pushing and pulling, backing and filling, and snorting and snaffling. The tender things they said to each other during the monolithic give-and-take of their courtship sounded as lyric to them as flowers in bud or green things opening. To the Greys, however, the bumbling romp of the lover and his lass was hard to comprehend and even harder to tolerate, and for a time they thought of calling the A.B.I., or African Bureau of Investigation, on the ground that monolithic lovemaking by enormous creatures who should have become decent fossils long ago

2 **coastwise:** längs der Küste, Küsten-.
3 **cargo:** Ladung.
waterlogged: voll Wasser gesogen, durchweicht.
5 **oblivious:** (fig.) blind, nicht gewahr.
scornful: verächtlich, hämisch.
6 **to bump:** rammen, stoßen.
8 **to back and fill** (AE, coll.): unschlüssig sein, schwanken.
to snort: schnauben.
to snaffle: im Zaum halten.
9f. **monolithic:** monolithisch, wie ein Steinblock.
10 **courtship:** Werbung.
11 **bud:** Knospe.
12 **to bumble:** sich tollpatschig bewegen.
romp: Tollen, Toben.
13 **to comprehend:** begreifen, verstehen.
15 **A.B.I.:** Anspielung auf *F.B.I.:* Abk. für *Federal Bureau of Investigation* (Bundeskriminalpolizei der USA).
17 **decent:** anständig.

was probably a threat to the security of the jungle. But they decided instead to phone their friends and neighbours and gossip about the shameless pair, and describe them in mocking and monstrous metaphors involving skidding buses on icy streets and overturned moving vans.

Late that evening, the hippopotamus and the hippopotama were surprised and shocked to hear the Greys exchanging terms of endearment. "Listen to those squawks," wuffled the male hippopotamus.

"What in the world can they see in each other?" gurbled the female hippopotamus.

"I would as soon live with a pair of unoiled garden shears," said her inamoratus.

They called up their friends and neighbours and discussed the incredible fact that a male grey parrot and a female grey parrot could possibly have any sex appeal. It was long after midnight before the hippopotamuses stopped criticizing the Greys and fell asleep, and the Greys

1 **jungle:** Dschungel, Urwald.
3 **to gossip:** klatschen, schwatzen.
4 **mocking:** spöttisch, höhnisch.
monstrous: ungeheuer, absurd.
metaphor: Metapher, bildlicher Ausdruck.
5 **to skid:** rutschen, schleudern.
overturned: umgestürzt.
5 f. **moving van:** Möbelwagen.
9 **term of endearment:** Kosewort.
10 **squawk:** Gekrächze.
10 f. **to wuffle / to gurble:** Beide Verben sind lautmalerische Wortschöpfungen Thurbers.
13 f. **garden shears** (pl.): Heckenschere.
14 **inamoratus:** Geliebter.

stopped maligning the hippopotamuses and retired to their beds.

MORAL: *Laugh and the world laughs with you, love and you love alone.*

The Private Life of Mr Bidwell

From where she was sitting, Mrs Bidwell could not see her husband, but she had a curious feeling of tension: she knew he was up to something.

"What are you doing, George?" she demanded, her eyes still on her book.

"Mm?"

"What's the matter with you?"

"Pahhhhh-h-h," said Mr Bidwell, in a long, pleasurable exhale. "I was holding my breath."

Mrs Bidwell twisted creakingly in her chair and looked at him; he was sitting behind her in his favourite place under the parchment lamp with the street scene of old

1 **to malign:** lästern; beschimpfen.
3 f. **Laugh . . . you love alone:** Anspielung auf eine bekannte Wendung aus dem Gedicht »Solitude« der Amerikanerin Ella Wheeler Wilcox (1850–1919): »Laugh, and the world laughs with you; / Weep, and you weep alone.«
7 **tension:** Spannung, Anspannung.
8 **to be up to s.th.:** etwas im Schilde führen, anstellen.
13 **pleasurable:** genüßlich.
14 **exhale:** Ausatmen.
15 **creakingly** (adv.): knarrend, quietschend.
17 **parchment lamp:** Lampe mit einem Schirm aus Pergament.

New York on it. "I was just holding my breath," he said again.

"Well, please don't do it," said Mrs Bidwell, and went back to her book. There was silence for five minutes.

"George!" said Mrs Bidwell.

"Bwaaaaaa," said Mr Bidwell. "What?"

"Will you please *stop* that?" she said. "It makes me nervous."

"I don't see how that bothers you," he said. "Can't I breathe?"

"You can breathe without holding your breath like a goop," said Mrs Bidwell. "Goop" was a word that she was fond of using; she rather lazily applied it to everything. It annoyed Mr Bidwell.

"Deep breathing," said Mr Bidwell, in the impatient tone he used when explaining anything to his wife, "is good exercise. You ought to take more exercise."

"Well, please don't do it around me," said Mrs Bidwell, turning again to the pages of Mr Galsworthy.

At the Cowans' party, a week later, the room was full of chattering people when Mrs Bidwell, who was talking to Lida Carroll, suddenly turned around as if she had been summoned. In a chair in a far corner of the room, Mr Bidwell was holding his breath. His chest was expanded,

9 **to bother:** stören.
12 **goop** (slang): Tölpel, Flegel.
17 **to take exercise:** sich Bewegung verschaffen.
19 **Galsworthy:** John G. (1867–1933), englischer Schriftsteller; bekannt vor allem durch den Romanzyklus *The Forsyte Saga* (1906–21).
21 **to chatter:** schwatzen, plappern.
23 **to summon:** rufen, auffordern.
24 **expanded:** gedehnt, geweitet.

his chin drawn in; there was a strange stare in his eyes, and his face was slightly empurpled. Mrs Bidwell moved into the line of his vision and gave him a sharp, penetrating look. He deflated slowly and looked away.

Later, in the car, after they had driven in silence a mile or more on the way home, Mrs Bidwell said, "It seems to me you might at least have the kindness not to hold your breath in other people's houses."

"I wasn't hurting anybody," said Mr Bidwell.

"You looked silly!" said his wife. "You looked perfectly crazy!" She was driving and she began to speed up, as she always did when excited or angry. "What do you suppose people thought – you sitting there all swelled up, with your eyes popping out?"

"I wasn't all swelled up," he said, angrily.

"You looked like a goop," she said. The car slowed down, sighed, and came to a complete, despondent stop.

"We're out of gas," said Mrs Bidwell. It was bitterly cold and nastily sleeting. Mr Bidwell took a long, deep breath.

The breathing situation in the Bidwell family reached a critical point when Mr Bidwell began to inhale in his

2 **empurpled:** purpurrot verfärbt.
3 **line of vision:** Gesichtsfeld.
3f. **penetrating:** durchdringend.
4 **to deflate:** Luft ablassen.
13 **swelled up:** aufgebläht.
14 **to pop out:** hervorquellen.
17 **despondent:** mutlos, verzagt.
19 **gas:** Benzin (AE).
20 **nastily** (adv.): unangenehm, scheußlich.
to sleet: graupeln, hageln.
22 **to inhale:** einatmen.

sleep, slowly, and exhale with a protracted, growling "woooooooo." Mrs Bidwell, ordinarily a sound sleeper (except on nights when she was sure burglars were getting in), would wake up and reach over and shake her husband. "George!" she would say.

"Hawwwwww," Mr Bidwell would say, thickly. "Wahs maa nah, hm?"

After he had turned over and gone back to sleep, Mrs Bidwell would lie awake, thinking.

One morning at breakfast she said, "George, I'm not going to put up with this another day. If you can't stop blowing up like a grampus, I'm going to leave you."

There was a slight, quick lift in Mr Bidwell's heart, but he tried to look surprised and hurt.

"All right," he said. "Let's not talk about it."

Mrs Bidwell buttered another piece of toast. She described to him the way he sounded in his sleep. He read the paper.

*

With considerable effort, Mr Bidwell kept from inflating his chest for about a week, but one night at the McNallys'

1 **to exhale:** ausatmen.
protracted: in die Länge gezogen.
to growl: knurren, grollen.
2 **sound:** fest, tief (Schlaf).
3 **burglar:** Einbrecher.
6 **thickly** (adv.): undeutlich, dumpf.
6f. **Wahs maa nah?:** *What's the matter now?:* Was ist denn schon wieder los?
11 **to put up with s.th.:** etwas ertragen, sich etwas gefallen lassen.
12 **grampus:** Delphin, Wal.
13 **lift:** (fig.) Erhebung, Aufschwung (AE).
19 **to inflate:** aufblasen, aufblähen.

he hit on the idea of seeing how many seconds he could hold his breath. He was rather bored by the McNallys' party, anyway. He began timing himself with his wrist-watch in a remote corner of the living-room. Mrs Bidwell, who was in the kitchen talking children and clothes with Bea McNally, left her abruptly and slipped back into the living-room. She stood quietly behind her husband's chair. He knew she was there, and tried to let out his breath imperceptibly.

"I see you," she said, in a low, cold tone. Mr Bidwell jumped up.

1 **to hit on an idea:** einen Einfall haben.
3 **to time o.s.:** sich stoppen.
3f. **wrist-watch:** Armbanduhr.
4 **remote:** abgelegen.
9 **imperceptibly** (adv.): unmerklich.

"Why don't you let me alone?" he demanded.

"Will you please lower your voice?" she said, smiling so that if anyone were looking he wouldn't think the Bidwells were arguing.

"I'm getting pretty damned tired of this," said Bidwell in a low voice.

"You've ruined my evening!" she whispered.

"You've ruined mine, too!" he whispered back. They knifed each other, from head to stomach, with their eyes.

"Sitting here like a goop, holding your breath," said Mrs Bidwell. "People will think you are an idiot." She laughed, turning to greet a lady who was approaching them.

Mr Bidwell sat in his office the next afternoon, a black, moist afternoon, tapping a pencil on his desk, and scowling. "All right, then, get out, get out!" he muttered. "What do I care?" He was visualizing the scene when Mrs Bidwell would walk out on him. After going through it several times, he returned to his work, feeling vaguely contented. He made up his mind to breathe any way he wanted to, no matter what she did. And, having come to this decision, he oddly enough, and quite without effort, lost interest in holding his breath.

Everything went rather smoothly at the Bidwells' for a month or so. Mr Bidwell didn't do anything to annoy his

9 **to knife:** (fig.) erdolchen, erstechen.
16 **to tap:** klopfen.
16f. **to scowl:** die Stirn runzeln, finster dreinschauen.
18 **to visualize:** sich vorstellen.
19 **to walk out on s.o.:** jdn. im Stich lassen, verlassen.
20 **vaguely** (adv.): unbestimmt, irgendwie.

wife beyond leaving his razor on her dressing-table and forgetting to turn out the hall light when he went to bed. Then there came the night of the Bentons' party.

Mr Bidwell, bored as usual, was sitting in a far corner of the room, breathing normally. His wife was talking animatedly with Beth Williamson about negligees. Suddenly her voice slowed and an uneasy look came into her eyes: George was up to something. She turned around and sought him out. To anyone but Mrs Bidwell he must have seemed like any husband sitting in a chair. But his wife's lips set tightly. She walked casually over to him.

"What are you doing?" she demanded.

"Hm?" he said, looking at her vacantly.

"What are you *doing*?" she demanded, again. He gave her a harsh, venomous look, which she returned.

"I'm multiplying numbers in my head," he said, slowly and evenly, "if you must know." In the prolonged, probing examination that they silently, without moving any muscles save those of their eyes, gave each other, it became solidly, frozenly apparent to both of them that

1 **dressing-table:** Toilettentisch.
7 **animatedly** (adv.): angeregt.
negligee: Negligé, leichter Morgenmantel.
10 **to seek s.o. out:** jdn. aufsuchen.
12 **casually** (adv.): beiläufig, zwanglos.
16 **harsh:** hart, gefühllos.
venomous: giftig, gehässig.
18 **evenly** (adv.): ruhig, gelassen.
prolonged: anhaltend.
18 f. **probing:** prüfend, forschend.
21 **solidly** (adv.): gründlich, deutlich.
frozenly (adv.): frostig; unumstößlich.

the end of their endurance had arrived. The curious bond that held them together snapped – rather more easily than either had supposed was possible. That night, while undressing for bed, Mr Bidwell calmly multiplied numbers in his head. Mrs Bidwell stared coldly at him for a few moments, holding a stocking in her hand; she didn't bother to berate him. He paid no attention to her. The thing was simply over.

George Bidwell lives alone now (his wife remarried). He never goes to parties any more, and his old circle of friends rarely sees him. The last time that any of them did see him, he was walking along a country road with the halting, uncertain gait of a blind man: he was trying to see how many steps he could take without opening his eyes.

The Rabbits Who Caused All the Trouble

Within the memory of the youngest child there was a family of rabbits who lived near a pack of wolves. The wolves announced that they did not like the way the rabbits were living. (The wolves were crazy about the way they themselves were living, because it was the only way to live.) One night several wolves were killed in an

1 **endurance:** Geduld.
2 **to snap:** zerreißen.
7 **to berate:** schimpfen, schelten.
13 **halting:** zögernd, unsicher.
gait: Gang(art).
17 **pack:** Rudel.
19 **to be crazy about s.th.:** für etwas begeistert, auf etwas versessen sein.

earthquake and this was blamed on the rabbits, for it is well known that rabbits pound on the ground with their hind legs and cause earthquakes. On another night one of the wolves was killed by a bolt of lightning and this was also blamed on the rabbits, for it is well known that lettuce-eaters cause lightning. The wolves threatened to civilize the rabbits if they didn't behave, and the rabbits decided to run away to a desert island. But the other animals, who lived at a great distance, shamed them, saying, "You must stay where you are and be brave. This is no world for escapists. If the wolves attack you, we will come to your aid, in all probability." So the rabbits continued to live near the wolves and one day there was a terrible flood which drowned a great many wolves. This was blamed on the rabbits, for it is well known that carrot-nibblers with long ears cause floods. The wolves descended on the rabbits, for their own good, and imprisoned them in a dark cave, for their own protection.

When nothing was heard about the rabbits for some weeks, the other animals demanded to know what had

1 **earthquake:** Erdbeben.
to blame s.th. on s.o.: jdm. die Schuld, Verantwortung für etwas zuschieben.
2 **to pound:** schlagen, trommeln.
3 **hind leg:** Hinterbein.
4 **bolt of lightning:** Blitz(strahl).
5 f. **lettuce-eater:** Kopfsalatfresser.
8 **desert:** öde, wüst, unbewohnt.
9 **to shame:** mit Scham erfüllen, beschämen.
11 **escapist:** Eskapist, jd., der vor der Wirklichkeit fliehen will.
14 **flood:** Überschwemmung.
15 f. **carrot-nibbler:** Karottenknabberer.
17 **to descend on s.o.:** jdn. überfallen, über jdn. herfallen.
for their own good: zu ihrem eigenen Wohl.

happened to them. The wolves replied that the rabbits had been eaten and since they had been eaten the affair was a purely internal matter. But the other animals warned that they might possibly unite against the wolves unless some reason was given for the destruction of the rabbits. So the wolves gave them one. "They were trying to escape," said the wolves, "and, as you know, this is no world for escapists."

MORAL: *Run, don't walk, to the nearest desert island.*

The Tiger Who Would Be King

One morning the tiger woke up in the jungle and told his mate that he was king of beasts.

"Leo, the lion, is king of beasts," she said.

"We need a change," said the tiger. "The creatures are crying for a change."

The tigress listened but she could hear no crying, except that of her cubs.

"I'll be king of beasts by the time the moon rises," said the tiger. "It will be a yellow moon with black stripes, in my honour."

"Oh, sure," said the tigress as she went to look after her

3 **internal matter:** innere Angelegenheit.
10 **would** (arch.): wollte.
11 **jungle:** Dschungel, Urwald.
12 **mate:** Gemahlin.
17 **cub:** Junges.

young, one of whom, a male, very like his father, had got an imaginary thorn in his paw.

The tiger prowled through the jungle till he came to the lion's den. "Come out," he roared, "and greet the king of beasts! The king is dead, long live the king!"

Inside the den, the lioness woke her mate. "The king is here to see you," she said.

"What king?" he inquired, sleepily.

"The king of beasts," she said.

"I am the king of beasts," roared Leo, and he charged out of the den to defend his crown against the pretender.

It was a terrible fight, and it lasted until the setting of the sun. All the animals of the jungle joined in, some taking the side of the tiger and others the side of the lion. Every creature from the aardvark to the zebra took part in the struggle to overthrow the lion or to repulse the tiger, and some did not know which they were fighting for, and some fought for both, and some fought whoever was nearest, and some fought for the sake of fighting.

"What are we fighting for?" someone asked the aardvark.

"The old order," said the aardvark.

"What are we dying for?" someone asked the zebra.

"The new order," said the zebra.

2 **imaginary:** nur in der Einbildung existierend.
3 **to prowl:** (auf der Suche nach Beute) herumschleichen, -streifen.
4 **den:** Höhle.
10 **to charge:** herbeistürmen, einen Angriff machen.
11 **pretender:** Prätendent, jd., der Anspruch auf einen Thron erhebt.
15 **aardvark:** Erdferkel (erstes Tier im Alphabet).
16 **to overthrow:** (fig.) stürzen.
to repulse: zurückschlagen, abweisen.

When the moon rose, fevered and gibbous, it shone upon a jungle in which nothing stirred except a macaw and a cockatoo, screaming in horror. All the beasts were dead except the tiger, and his days were numbered and his time was ticking away. He was monarch of all he surveyed, but it didn't seem to mean anything.

MORAL: *You can't very well be king of beasts if there aren't any.*

The Admiral on the Wheel

When the coloured maid stepped on my glasses the other morning, it was the first time they had been broken since the late Thomas A. Edison's seventy-ninth birthday. I remember that day well, because I was working for a newspaper then and I had been assigned to go over to West Orange that morning and interview Mr Edison. I got up early and, in reaching for my glasses under the bed (where I always put them), I found that one of my more

1 **fevered:** fiebernd, fieberhaft.
gibbous: auf beiden Seiten konvex (Mondscheibe zwischen Halb- und Vollmond).
2 **macaw:** Ara, Keilschwanzsittich.
3 **cockatoo:** Kakadu.
9 **wheel** (AE, coll.): Fahrrad.
12 **Edison:** Thomas Alva E. (1847–1931), amerikanischer Erfinder; feierte seinen neunundsiebzigsten Geburtstag am 11. Februar 1926.
14 **to assign:** beauftragen, bestimmen.
15 **West Orange:** Stadt im US-Bundesstaat New Jersey, Sitz des Edison Laboratory.

sober and reflective Scotch terriers was quietly chewing them. Both tortoiseshell temples (the pieces that go over your ears) had been eaten and Jeannie was toying with the lenses in a sort of jaded way. It was in going over to Jersey that day, without my glasses, that I realized that the disadvantages of defective vision (bad eyesight) are at least partially compensated for by its peculiar advantages. Up to that time I had been in the habit of going to bed when my glasses were broken and lying there until they were fixed again. I had believed I could not go very far without them, not more than a block, anyway, on account of the danger of bumping into things, getting a headache, losing my way. None of those things happened, but a lot of others did. I saw the Cuban flag flying over a national bank, I saw a gay old lady with a grey parasol walk right through the side of a truck, I saw a cat roll across a street in a small striped barrel, I saw bridges rise lazily into the air, like balloons.

I suppose you have to have just the right proportion of

1 **sober:** gesetzt, vernünftig.
reflective: nachdenklich, beschaulich.
2 **tortoiseshell:** Schildpatt.
temple: Brillenbügel.
3 **to toy:** spielen.
4 **lens:** (Brillen-)Glas.
jaded: erschöpft, übersättigt.
6 **defective:** mangelhaft.
vision: Sehvermögen.
eyesight: Sehkraft.
10 **to fix:** reparieren.
12 **to bump into s.th.:** an etwas stoßen, mit etwas zusammenstoßen.
16 **parasol:** Sonnenschirm.
truck: Lastwagen, LKW (AE).
19 **proportion:** Ausmaß, Grad.

sight to encounter such phenomena: I seem to remember that oculists have told me I have only two-fifths vision without what one of them referred to as "artificial compensation" (glasses). With three-fifths vision or better, I suppose the Cuban flag would have been an American flag, the gay old lady a garbage man with a garbage can on his back, the cat a piece of butcher's paper blowing in the wind, the floating bridges smoke from tugs, hanging in the air. With perfect vision, one is extricably trapped in the workaday world, a prisoner of reality, as lost in the commonplace America of 1937 as Alexander Selkirk was lost on his lonely island. For the hawk-eyed person life has none of those soft edges which for me blur into fantasy; for such a person an electric welder is merely an electric welder, not a radiant fool setting off a sky-rocket by day. The kingdom of the partly blind is a little like

1 **phenomenon** (pl. *phenomena*): Erscheinung, Wunder.
2 **oculist:** Augenarzt, -spezialist.
4–6 **I suppose the Cuban flag would have been an American flag:** Die kubanische Flagge zeigt horizontale, blaue und weiße Streifen und links ein rotes Dreieck mit weißem Stern.
6 **garbage man:** Müllmann (AE).
garbage can: Mülltonne (AE).
8 **to float:** schweben.
tug: Schlepper.
9 **extricably** (adv.): *inextricably:* unauflösbar.
10 **workaday:** werktäglich, alltäglich.
11 **commonplace:** alltäglich, gewöhnlich.
Selkirk: Alexander S. (1676–1721), schottischer Seemann; historisches Vorbild für Robinson Crusoe.
12 **hawk-eyed:** scharfsichtig, mit Falkenaugen.
13 **to blur:** verschwimmen.
14 **welder:** Schweißer.
15 **radiant:** strahlend, leuchtend.
sky-rocket: Feuerwerksrakete.

Oz, a little like Wonderland, a little like Poictesme. Anything you can think of, and a lot you never would think of, can happen there.

For three days after the maid, in cleaning the apartment, stepped on my glasses – I had not put them far enough under the bed – I worked at home and did not go uptown to have them fixed. It was in this period that I made the acquaintance of a remarkable Chesapeake spaniel. I looked out of my window and after a moment spotted him, a noble, silent dog lying on a ledge above the entrance to a brownstone house in lower Fifth Avenue. He lay there, proud and austere, for three days and nights, sleepless, never eating, the perfect watchdog. No ordinary dog could have got up on the high ledge above the doorway, to begin with; no ordinary people would have owned such an animal. The ordinary people were the people who walked by the house and did not see the dog. Oh, I got my glasses fixed finally and I know that now the dog has gone, but I haven't looked to see what prosaic

1 **Oz:** Zauberreich des volkstümlichen Kinderbuchs *The Wonderful Wizard of Oz* (1900) des amerikanischen Schriftstellers Lyman Frank Baum (1856–1919).
Wonderland: Anspielung auf *Alice in Wonderland* (1865) des englischen Schriftstellers Lewis Carroll (d. i. Charles Lutwidge Dodgson, 1832–98).
Poictesme: Phantasiereich an der französischen Mittelmeerküste zur Zeit des Hochmittelalters, das in den Romanen des amerikanischen Schriftstellers James Branch Cabell (1879–1958) eine große Rolle spielt; sein bekanntestes Werk ist *Jurgen. A Comedy of Justice* (1919).
8 **Chesapeake spaniel:** Hunderasse.
9 **to spot:** erkennen, entdecken.
10 **ledge:** Sims.
11 **brownstone:** brauner Sandstein.
12 **austere:** abweisend.
19 **prosaic:** prosaisch, alltäglich.

object occupies the spot where he so staunchly stood guard over one of the last of the old New York houses on Fifth Avenue; perhaps an unpainted flower-box or a cleaning cloth dropped from an upper window by a careless menial. The moment of disenchantment would be too hard; I never look out of that particular window any more.

Sometimes at night, even with my glasses on, I see strange and unbelievable sights, mainly when I am riding in an automobile which somebody else is driving (I never drive myself at night out of fear that I might turn up at the portals of some mystical monastery and never return). Only last summer I was riding with someone along a country road when suddenly I cried at him to look out. He slowed down and asked me sharply what was the matter. There is no worse experience than to have someone shout at you to look out for something you don't see. What this driver didn't see and I did see (two-fifths vision works a kind of magic in the night) was a little old admiral in full-dress uniform riding a bicycle at right angles to the car I was in. He might have been starlight behind a tree, or a billboard advertising Moxie; I don't know – we were quickly past the place he rode out of; but I would recognize him if I saw him again. His beard was blowing in the

1 **staunchly** (adv.): treu, zuverlässig.
5 **menial:** Hausangestellte(r).
disenchantment: Ernüchterung, Desillusionierung.
12 **portal:** Portal, Pforte, Tor.
mystical: mystisch, geheimnisvoll.
monastery: Kloster.
20 **full-dress uniform:** Galauniform.
22 **billboard:** Anschlagtafel (AE).
Moxie: Handelsname eines alkoholfreien Mixgetränks.

breeze and his hat was set at a rakish angle, like Admiral Beatty's. He was having a swell time. The gentleman who was driving the car has been, since that night, a trifle stiff and distant with me. I suppose you can hardly blame him.

To go back to my daylight experiences with the naked eye, it was me, in case you have heard the story, who once killed fifteen white chickens with small stones. The poor beggars never had a chance. This happened many

1 **rakish:** schmissig, verwegen.

2 **Beatty:** David, Earl B. of the North Sea and of Brooksby (1871 bis 1936), britischer Admiral; befehligte die englischen Streitkräfte in den Seegefechten bei Helgoland und im Skagerrak.
to have a swell time: sich toll, prima amüsieren.

3 **a trifle:** ein bißchen, etwas.

4 **distant:** kühl, zurückhaltend.

7f. **who once killed fifteen white chickens with small stones:** Verballhornung der Redewendung *to kill two birds with one stone* ›zwei Fliegen mit einer Klappe schlagen‹.

9 **poor beggars:** arme Teufel.

years ago when I was living at Jay, New York. I had a vegetable garden some seventy feet behind the house, and the lady of the house had asked me to keep an eye on it in my spare moments and to chase away any chickens from neighbouring farms that came pecking around. One morning, getting up from my typewriter, I wandered out behind the house and saw that a flock of white chickens had invaded the garden. I had, to be sure, misplaced my glasses for the moment, but I could still see well enough to let the chickens have it with ammunition from a pile of stones that I kept handy for the purpose. Before I could be stopped, I had riddled all the tomato plants in the garden, over the tops of which the lady of the house had, the twilight before, placed newspapers and paper bags to ward off the effects of frost. It was one of the darker experiences of my dimmer hours.

Some day, I suppose, when the clouds are heavy and the rain is coming down and the pressure of realities is too great, I shall deliberately take my glasses off and go wandering out into the streets. I dare say I may never be heard of again (I have always believed it was Ambrose Bierce's vision and not his whim that caused him to wander into oblivion). I imagine I'll have a remarkable time, wherever I end up.

5 **to peck:** picken, hacken.
11 **handy:** griffbereit.
12 **to riddle:** durchlöchern, durchsieben.
14 **twilight:** Dämmerung.
15 **to ward off:** abwehren, abwenden.
22 **Bierce:** Ambrose B. (1842–1914), amerikanischer Journalist und Autor brillanter Kurzgeschichten; im mexikanischen Krieg verschollen. **whim:** Laune, Grille.
23 **oblivion:** Vergessen(heit).
24 **to end up:** (fig.) landen; sterben.

The Little Girl and the Wolf

One afternoon a big wolf waited in a dark forest for a little girl to come along carrying a basket of food to her grandmother. Finally a little girl did come along and she was carrying a basket of food. "Are you carrying that basket to your grandmother?" asked the wolf. The little girl said yes, she was. So the wolf asked her where her

grandmother lived and the little girl told him and he disappeared into the wood.

When the little girl opened the door of her grandmother's house she saw that there was somebody in bed with a nightcap and nightgown on. She had approached no nearer than twenty-five feet from the bed when she saw that it was not her grandmother but the wolf, for even in a nightcap a wolf does not look any more like your grandmother than the Metro-Goldwyn lion looks like Calvin Coolidge. So the little girl took an automatic out of her basket and shot the wolf dead.

MORAL: *It is not so easy to fool little girls nowadays as it used to be.*

The Peacelike Mongoose

In cobra country a mongoose was born one day who didn't want to fight cobras or anything else. The word spread from mongoose to mongoose that there was a

5 **nightcap:** Nachtmütze.
nightgown: Nachthemd.
9 **Metro-Goldwyn lion:** Firmenzeichen der Metro-Goldwyn-Mayer-Filmgesellschaft.
10 **Coolidge:** Calvin C. (1872–1933), Präsident der USA von 1923 bis 1930.
automatic: automatische Pistole.
12 **to fool s.o.:** jdn. zum Narren halten, hinters Licht führen.
14 **peacelike:** friedliebend.
mongoose: Mungo.

mongoose who didn't want to fight cobras. If he didn't want to fight anything else, it was his own business, but it was the duty of every mongoose to kill cobras or be killed by cobras.

"Why?" asked the peacelike mongoose, and the word went around that the strange new mongoose was not only pro-cobra and anti-mongoose but intellectually curious and against the ideals and traditions of mongoosism.

"He is crazy," cried the young mongoose's father.

"He is sick," said his mother.

"He is a coward," shouted his brothers.

"He is a mongoosexual," whispered his sisters.

Strangers who had never laid eyes on the peacelike mongoose remembered that they had seen him crawling on his stomach, or trying on cobra hoods, or plotting the violent overthrow of Mongoosia.

"I am trying to use reason and intelligence," said the strange new mongoose.

"Reason is six-sevenths of treason," said one of his neighbours.

"Intelligence is what the enemy uses," said another.

Finally, the rumour spread that the mongoose had venom in his sting, like a cobra, and he was tried,

12 **mongoosexual:** Wortschöpfung aus *homosexual* und *mongoose*.
15 **hood:** Haube, Überwurf.
to plot: (Verschwörung) planen.
16 **overthrow:** (fig.) Sturz.
19 **treason:** Verrat.
21 **intelligence:** hier: Spionage.
22 **rumour:** Gerücht.
23 **venom:** Gift.
sting: hier: Biß.
to try: vor Gericht stellen, verhören.

convicted by a show of paws, and condemned to banishment.

MORAL: *Ashes to ashes, and clay to clay, if the enemy doesn't get you your own folks may.*

The Wolf Who Went Places

A wealthy young wolf, who was oblivious of everything except himself, was tossed out of college for cutting classes and corners, and he decided to see if he could travel around the world in eighty minutes.

"That isn't possible," his grandmother told him, but he only grinned at her.

"The impossible is the most fun," he said.

She went with him to the door of the old Wolf place. "If you go that fast, you won't live to regret it," she warned him, but he grinned again, showing a tongue as long as a necktie.

1 **to convict:** überführen, für schuldig erklären.
show of paws: Wortschöpfung zu *show of hands* ›Handzeichen‹.
1 f. **banishment:** Verbannung.
3 **ashes to ashes:** Anspielung auf die Bestattungsliturgie: »Ashes to ashes, dust to dust«.
clay: irdische Hülle, Erde.
5 **to go places:** weit herumkommen; erfolgreich sein.
6 **to be oblivious of s.th.:** etwas vergessen (haben), blind für etwas sein.
7 **to toss out:** hinauswerfen, -schmeißen.
7 f. **to cut classes:** Schule schwänzen.
to cut corners: Weg abschneiden.
11 **to grin at s.o.:** jdn. angrinsen.
16 **necktie:** Krawatte.

"That's an old wolves' tale," he said, and went on his reckless way.

He bought a 1959 Blitzen Bearcat, a combination motorcar and airplane, with skyrocket getaway, cyclone speeddrive, cannonball takeoff, blindall headlights, magical retractable monowings, and lightning pushbutton transformationizer. "How fast can this crate go without burning up?" he asked the Blitzen Bearcat salesman.

"I don't know," the salesman said, "but I have a feeling you'll find out."

The wealthy young wolf smashed all the ground records and air records and a lot of other things in his trip around the world, which took him only 78.5 minutes from the time he knocked down the Washington Monument on his takeoff to the time he landed where it had stood. In the crowd that welcomed him home, consisting of about eleven creatures, for all the others were hiding under beds,

1 **old wolves' tale:** Wortschöpfung zu *old wives' tale* ›Altweibergeschwätz, Ammenmärchen‹.
2 **reckless:** leichtsinnig, unbekümmert.
3 **Blitzen Bearcat:** nach den Rennwagen Blitzen Ben und Stutz Bearcat (1910/11).
4 **skyrocket:** Feuerwerksrakete.
getaway: Abzug (Auto).
cyclone: Wirbelsturm, Tornado.
4 f. **speeddrive:** Hochgeschwindigkeitsantrieb.
5 **takeoff:** Start.
blindall headlights: alles blendende Scheinwerfer.
6 **retractable:** einziehbar.
monowing: Monotragfläche.
pushbutton: durch Knopfdruck steuerbar, automatisch.
6 f. **transformationizer:** Wortschöpfung (von *to transform* ›umwandeln‹).
7 **crate** (slang): ‚Kiste' (Auto, Flugzeug).
11 **to smash a record:** einen Rekord brechen.

there was a speed-crazy young wolfess, with built-in instantaneous pickup ability, and in no time at all the wolf and his new-found mate were setting new records for driving upside down, backward, blindfolded, handcuffed, and cockeyed, doubled and redoubled.

One day, they decided to see if they could turn in to Central Park from Fifth Avenue while travelling at a rate of 175 miles an hour, watching television, and holding hands. There was a tremendous shattering, crashing, splitting, roaring, blazing, cracking, and smashing, ending in a fiery display of wheels, stars, cornices, roofs, treetops, glass, steel, and people, and it seemed to those spectators who did not die of seizures as they watched the great red portals opened in the sky, swinging inward on mighty hinges, revealing an endless nowhere, and then

1 **speed-crazy:** dem Geschwindigkeitsrausch verfallen.
2 **instantaneous:** sofortig, blitzschnell.
pickup ability: Anzugsvermögen, Starteigenschaften (*to pick up:* [ein Mädchen] ‚aufgabeln', ‚aufreißen').
3 **mate:** Gefährtin, Freundin.
4 **upside down:** verkehrt herum.
4f. **blindfolded:** mit verbundenen Augen.
5 **handcuffed:** in Handschellen.
cockeyed: schielend; betrunken.
5f. **to double and redouble:** wieder und wieder umkehren.
10 **shattering:** Schmettern, Krachen.
11 **blazing:** Aufflammen, Lodern.
cracking: Krachen, Knallen; Zerspringen.
12 **fiery:** glühend, feurig.
display: Schauspiel.
cornice: Gesims.
14 **seizure:** Anfall.
15 **portal** (poet.): Tür, Pforte.
16 **hinge:** Angel, Scharnier.

closed behind the flying and flaming wolves with a clanking to end all clanking, as if those gates which we have been assured shall not prevail had, in fact, prevailed.

MORAL: *Where most of us end up there is no knowing, but the hellbent get where they are going.*

The Macbeth Murder Mystery

"It was a stupid mistake to make," said the American woman I had met at my hotel in the English lake country, "but it was on the counter with the other Penguin books – the little sixpenny ones, you know, with the paper covers – and I supposed of course it was a detective story. All the others were detective stories. I'd read all the others, so I bought this one without really looking at it carefully. You can imagine how mad I was when I found it was Shakespeare." I murmured something sympathetically.

1 f. **clanking:** Geklirr, Gerassel.
3 **to prevail:** (ob)siegen, sich behaupten; Anspielung auf Mt. 16,18: »and the gates of hell shall not prevail against it« (»und die Pforten der Hölle sollen sie [die Kirche] nicht überwältigen«).
4 **to end up:** (fig.) landen; sterben.
5 **hellbent** (slang): jd., der wild hinter etwas her ist; wörtl.: jd., der sich auf dem Weg zur Hölle befindet.
8 **English lake country:** Seengebiet im Nordwesten Englands.
9 **Penguin books:** englischer Taschenbuchverlag mit einem Pinguin als Warenzeichen.
14 **mad** (coll.): verärgert, wütend.
15 **sympathetically** (adv.): verständnis-, teilnahmsvoll.

"I don't see why the Penguin-books people had to get out Shakespeare's plays in the same size and everything as the detective stories," went on my companion. "I think they have different-coloured jackets," I said. "Well, I didn't notice that," she said. "Anyway, I got real comfy in bed that night and all ready to read a good mystery story and here I had 'The Tragedy of Macbeth' – a book for high-school students. Like 'Ivanhoe.' " "Or 'Lorna Doone'," I said. "Exactly," said the American lady. "And I was just crazy for a good Agatha Christie, or something. Hercule Poirot is my favourite detective." "Is he the rabbity one?" I asked. "Oh, no," said my crime-fiction expert. "He's the Belgian one. You're thinking of Mr Pinkerton, the one that helps Inspector Bull. He's good, too." Over her second cup of tea my companion began to tell the plot of a detective story that had fooled her completely – it seems it was the old family doctor all the time. But I cut in on her. "Tell me," I said. "Did you read

4 **jacket:** Umschlag.
5 **comfy** (coll.): gemütlich, behaglich.
8 **'Ivanhoe':** Titel eines 1819 erschienenen, weithin bekannten historischen Romans des englischen Schriftstellers Sir Walter Scott (1771–1832).
'Lorna Doone': Titel eines 1869 erschienenen, melodramatischen Liebes- und Abenteuerromans des englischen Dichters Richard Doddridge Blackmore (1825–1900); gilt als der populärste Trivialroman der viktorianischen Ära.
11 **rabbity:** ängstlich, scheu.
12 **crime-fiction:** Kriminalroman(e).
13/14 **Pinkerton / Bull:** Evan Pinkerton und Inspector J. Humphrey Bull sind Figuren aus den Kriminalromanen von David Frome (d. i. Zenith Jones Brown, geb. 1898, die auch unter dem Pseudonym Leslie Ford schrieb).
16 **to fool s.o.:** jdn. zum Narren halten, hinters Licht führen.
18 **to cut in on s.o.:** jdn. unterbrechen, jdm. ins Wort fallen.

'Macbeth'?" "I *had* to read it," she said. "There wasn't a scrap of anything else to read in the whole room." "Did you like it?" I asked. "No, I did not," she said, decisively. "In the first place, I don't think for a moment that Macbeth did it." I looked at her blankly. "Did what?" I asked. "I don't think for a moment that he killed the King," she said. "I don't think the Macbeth woman was mixed up in it, either. You suspect them the most, of course, but those are the ones that are never guilty – or shouldn't be, anyway." "I'm afraid," I began, "that I –" "But don't you see?" said the American lady. "It would spoil everything if you could figure out right away who did it. Shakespeare was too smart for that. I've read that people never *have* figured out 'Hamlet,' so it isn't likely Shakespeare would have made 'Macbeth' as simple as it seems." I thought this over while I filled my pipe. "Who do you suspect?" I asked, suddenly. "Macduff," she said, promptly. "Good God!" I whispered, softly.

"Oh, Macduff did it, all right," said the murder specialist. "Hercule Poirot would have got him easily." "How did you figure it out?" I demanded. "Well," she said, "I

1f. **not a scrap:** nichts, kein bißchen (*scrap:* Fetzen, Stück).

3 **decisively** (adv.): entschieden.

4f. **I don't think . . . Macbeth did it:** Die doppeldeutigen Prophezeiungen der drei Hexen und die Einflüsterungen seiner ehrgeizigen Gemahlin verführen Macbeth, den siegreichen General des schottischen Königs Duncan, dazu, diesen zu ermorden.

5 **blankly** (adv.): hier: verblüfft.

12 **to figure out** (coll.): (sich) ausrechnen, herausfinden.

13 **smart:** klug, pfiffig.

17f. **Macduff:** Gefolgsmann König Duncans, der Macbeth tötet (*Macbeth* V,8).

didn't right away. At first I suspected Banquo. And then, of course, he was the second person killed. That was good right in there, that part. The person you suspect of the first murder should always be the second victim." "Is that so?" I murmured. "Oh, yes," said my informant. "They have to keep surprising you. Well, after the second murder I didn't know *who* the killer was for a while." "How about Malcolm and Donalbain, the King's sons?" I asked. "As I remember it, they fled right after the first murder. That looks suspicious." "Too suspicious," said the American lady. "Much too suspicious. When they flee, they're never guilty. You can count on that." "I believe," I said, "I'll have a brandy," and I summoned the waiter. My companion leaned toward me, her eyes bright, her teacup quivering. "Do you know who discovered Duncan's body?" she demanded. I said I was sorry, but I had forgotten. "Macduff dicovers it," she said, slipping into the historical present. "Then he comes running downstairs and shouts, 'Confusion has broke open the Lord's anointed temple' and 'Sacrilegious murder has made his masterpiece' and on and on like that." The

1 **Banquo:** General Duncans, den Macbeth von gedungenen Mördern töten läßt, da die drei Hexen prophezeiten, Banquo würde Könige zeugen.

5 **informant:** Gewährsmännin.

13 **to summon:** (herbei)rufen.

15 **to quiver:** zittern.

18 **historical present:** historisches Präsens.

19–21 **Confusion . . . made his masterpiece:** Thurber läßt die Amerikanerin falsch zitieren; *Macbeth* II,3,66 ff. lautet: »Confusion now hath made his masterpiece! / Most sacrilegious murther hath broke ope / The Lord's anointed temple« (*sacrilegious:* entweihend, frevelhaft; *anointed:* gesalbt; *temple:* 1. Tempel [gemeint ist Duncans Körper]; 2. Schläfe).

good lady tapped me on the knee. "All that stuff was *rehearsed*," she said. "You wouldn't say a lot of stuff like that, offhand, would you – if you had found a body?" She fixed me with a glittering eye. "I —" I began. "You're right!" she said. "You wouldn't! Unless you had practised it in advance. 'My God, there's a body in here!' is what an innocent man would say." She sat back with a confident glare.

I thought for a while. "But what do you make of the Third Murderer?" I asked. "You know, the Third Murderer has puzzled 'Macbeth' scholars for three hundred years." "That's because they never thought of Macduff," said the American lady. "It was Macduff, I'm certain. You couldn't have one of the victims murdered by two ordinary thugs – the murderer always has to be somebody important." "But what about the banquet scene?" I asked, after a moment. "How do you account for Macbeth's guilty actions there, when Banquo's ghost came in and sat in his chair?" The lady leaned forward and tapped me on the knee again. "There wasn't any ghost," she said. "A big, strong man like that doesn't go around seeing ghosts – especially in a brightly lighted banquet hall with dozens of people around. Macbeth was *shielding somebody!*" "Who was he shielding?" I asked. "Mrs

1 **to tap:** klopfen.
2 **to rehearse:** einstudieren, proben.
3 **offhand:** einfach so, leichthin.
8 **glare:** wilder, funkelnder Blick.
10 **Third Murderer:** Manche Literaturkritiker vermuten, daß in einer längeren Fassung des Stückes eine Szene existierte, die die Gegenwart des dritten Mörders in III,3 erklärt.
15 **thug:** Mörder, Schurke.
16 **banquet scene:** Bankettszene (*Macbeth* III,4).
23 f. **to shield:** decken, schützen.

Macbeth, of course," she said. "He thought she did it and he was going to take the rap himself. The husband always does that when the wife is suspected." "But what," I demanded, "about the sleepwalking scene, then?" "The same thing, only the other way around," said my companion. "That time *she* was shielding *him*. She wasn't asleep at all. Do you remember where it says, 'Enter Lady Macbeth with a taper'?" "Yes," I said. "Well, people who walk in their sleep *never carry lights!*" said my fellow-traveller. "They have second sight. Did you ever hear of a sleepwalker carrying a light?" "No," I said, "I never did." "Well, then, she wasn't asleep. She was acting guilty to shield Macbeth." "I think," I said, "I'll have another brandy," and I called the waiter. When he brought it, I drank it rapidly and rose to go. "I believe," I said, "that you have got hold of something. Would you lend me that 'Macbeth'? I'd like to look it over tonight. I don't feel, somehow, as if I'd ever really read it." "I'll get it for you," she said. "But you'll find that I am right."

*

I read the play over carefully that night, and the next morning, after breakfast, I sought out the American woman. She was on the putting green, and I came up behind her silently and took her arm. She gave an excla-

2 **to take the rap:** die Schuld auf sich nehmen.
4 **sleepwalking scene:** Szene des Nachtwandelns (*Macbeth* V,1).
8 **taper:** Fackel.
10 **second sight:** zweites Gesicht, Hellsehen.
21 **to seek out:** (auf)suchen.
22 **putting green:** Grün (Teil des Golfplatzes innerhalb eines Radius von 20 Yards vom Loch aus); Rasenstück zum Üben des Puttens (*to putt:* putten, den Golfball mit vorsichtigem Schlag zum Loch treiben).

mation. "Could I see you alone?" I asked, in a low voice. She nodded cautiously and followed me to a secluded spot. "You've found out something?" she breathed. "I've found out," I said, triumphantly, "the name of the murderer!" "You mean it wasn't Macduff?" she said. "Macduff is as innocent of those murders," I said, "as Macbeth and the Macbeth woman." I opened the copy of the play, which I had with me, and turned to Act II, Scene 2. "Here," I said, "you will see where Lady Macbeth says, 'I laid their daggers ready. He could not miss 'em. Had he not resembled my father as he slept, I had done it.' Do you see?" "No," said the American woman, bluntly, "I don't." "But it's simple!" I exclaimed. "I wonder I didn't see it years ago. The reason Duncan resembled Lady Macbeth's father as he slept is that *it actually was her father!*" "Good God!" breathed my companion, softly. "Lady Macbeth's father killed the King," I said, "and, hearing someone coming, thrust the body under the bed and crawled into the bed himself." "But," said the lady, "you can't have a murderer who only appears in the story once. You can't have that." "I know that," I said, and I turned to Act II, Scene 4. "It says here, 'Enter Ross with an old Man.' Now, that old man is never identified and it is my contention he was old Mr Macbeth, whose ambition it was to make his daughter Queen. There you have your motive." "But even then," cried the American lady, "he's still a minor character!" "Not," I

10 **dagger:** Dolch.
13 **bluntly** (adv.): offen.
18 **to thrust:** schieben, stecken.
23 **Ross:** richtig: *Rosse:* schottischer Edelmann.
24 **contention:** Argument, Behauptung.

said, gleefully, "when you realize that he was also *one of the weird sisters in disguise!*" "You mean one of the three witches?" "Precisely," I said. "Listen to this speech of the old man's. 'On Tuesday last, a falcon towering in her pride of place, was by a mousing owl hawk'd at and kill'd.' Who does that sound like?" "It sounds like the way the three witches talk," said my companion, reluctantly. "Precisely!" I said again. "Well," said the American woman, "maybe you're right, but —" "I'm sure I am," I said. "And do you know what I'm going to do now?" "No," she said. "What?" "Buy a copy of 'Hamlet'," I said, "and solve *that*!" My companion's eyes brightened. "Then," she said, "you don't think Hamlet did it?" "I am," I said, "absolutely positive he didn't." "But who," she demanded, "do you suspect?" I looked at her cryptically. "Everybody," I said, and disappeared into a small grove of trees as silently as I had come.

1 **gleefully** (adv.): heiter, fröhlich.

2 **the weird sisters:** die Schicksalsschwestern, die (drei) Hexen; vgl. *Macbeth* I,3,32 (*weird* [poet.]: schicksalsbestimmend).

4–6 **'On Tuesday last . . . hawk'd at and kill'd':** *Macbeth* II,4,11 ff.: »Am letzten Dienstag sah ich, wie stolzen Flugs ein Falke schwebte und eine Eul' ihm nachjagt' und ihn würgte.«

7 f. **reluctantly** (adv.): zögernd, widerstrebend.

14 **positive:** sicher.

16 **cryptically** (adv.): rätselhaft, dunkel.

17 **grove:** Gehölz.

The Last Clock

A Fable for the Time, such as it is, of Man

In a country the other side of tomorrow, an ogre who had eaten a clock and had fallen into the habit of eating clocks was eating a clock in the clockroom of his castle when his ogress and their ilk knocked down the locked door and shook their hairy heads at him.

"Wulsa malla?" gurgled the ogre, for too much clock oil had turned all his "t"s to "l"s.

"Just look at this room!" exclaimed the ogress, and they all looked at the room, the ogre with eyes as fogged as the headlights of an ancient limousine. The stone floor of the room was littered with fragments of dials, oily coils and springs, broken clock hands, and pieces of pendulums. "I've brought a doctor to look at you," the ogress said.

The doctor wore a black beard, carried a black bag, and

2 **such as it is:** wie sie nun einmal ist.
3 **ogre:** Menschenfresser, Riese.
5 **clockroom:** Wortspiel mit *clock* und *cloakroom* ›Garderobe‹.
6 **ilk:** Familie, Art, Nachkommenschaft.
8 **Wulsa malla?:** *What's the matter?*
to gurgle: gurgeln, glucksen.
11 **fogged:** umnebelt, verdüstert.
12 **headlights** (pl.): Scheinwerfer.
13 **to litter:** übersäen, verunreinigen.
dial: Zifferblatt.
14 **coil:** Spiralfeder.
spring: Feder.
hand: Zeiger.
15 **pendulum:** Pendel.

gave the ogre a black look. "This case is clearly not in my area," he said.

The ogre struck three, and the doctor flushed.

"This is a case for a clockman," the doctor said, "for the problem is not what clocks have done to the ogre but what the ogre has done to clocks."

"Wulsa malla?" the ogre gurgled again.

"Eating clocks has turned all his 't's to 'l's," the ogress said. "That's what clocks have done to him."

"Then your clockman may have to call in consultation a semanticist or a dictionist or an etymologist or a syntaxman," the non-clock doctor said, and he bowed stiffly and left the room.

The next morning, the ogress brought into the clockroom a beardless man with a box of tools under his arm. "I've brought a clockman to see you," she told the ogre.

"No, no, no," said the beardless man with the box of tools. "I'm not a clockman. I thought you said clogman. I'm a clogman. I cannot ethically depart from my area, which is clogged drains and gutters. I get mice out of

1 **black look:** düsterer, unheilvoller Blick.
2 **area:** (Fach-)Gebiet; Branche, Geschäftszweig.
3 **to flush:** erröten.
10 **to call in consultation:** Rücksprache halten.
11 **semanticist:** Fachmann auf dem Gebiet der Semantik (Wortbedeutungslehre).
dictionist: Vortrags-, Aussprachespezialist (Wortschöpfung, abgeleitet von *diction* ›Ausdrucksweise, Stil‹).
etymologist: Etymologe (Wortforscher).
11 f. **syntaxman:** Spezialist auf dem Gebiet der Syntax (Satzbaulehre).
18 **clogman:** Spezialist für verstopfte Leitungen (Wortschöpfung, abgeleitet von *to clog* ›verstopfen‹).
19 **ethically** (adv.): hier: dem Berufsethos entsprechend.
20 **drain:** Kanalisation(srohr).
gutter: Abwasserkanal.

pipes, and bugs out of tubes, and moles out of tiles, and there my area ends." The clogman bowed and went away.

"Wuld wuzzle?" the ogre wanted to know. He hiccuped, and something went *spong!*

"That was an area man, but the wrong area," the ogress explained. "I'll get a general practitioner." And she went away and came back with a general practitioner.

"This is a waste of time," he said. "As a general practitioner, modern style, I treat only generals. This patient is not even a private. He sounds to me like a public place – a clock tower, perhaps, or a belfry."

"What shall I do?" asked the ogress. "Send for a tower man, or a belfry man?"

"I shall not venture an opinion," the general practitioner said. "I am a specialist in generals, one of whom has just lost command of his army and of all his faculties, and doesn't know what time it is. Good day." And the general practitioner went away.

The ogre cracked a small clock, as if it were a large walnut, and began eating it. "Wulsy wul?" the ogre asked.

1 **bug:** Ungeziefer.
mole: Maulwurf.
tile: hier: Tonrohr für einen Kanal.
4/21 **Wuld wuzzle? / Wulsy wul?:** unverständliche Äußerungen.
to hiccup: Schluckauf haben.
7 **general practitioner:** praktischer Arzt.
11 **private:** gemeiner Soldat.
12 **belfry:** Glockenturm.
15 **to venture:** wagen, riskieren.
17 **faculty:** Fähigkeit; (jur.) Befugnis.
20 **to crack:** auf-, zerknacken.
21 **walnut:** Walnuß.

The ogress, who could now talk clocktalk fluently, even oilily, but wouldn't, left the room to look up specialists in an enormous volume entitled "Who's Who in Areas." She soon became lost in a list of titles: clockmaker, clocksmith, clockwright, clockmonger, clockician, clockometrist, clockologist, and a hundred others dealing with clockness, clockism, clockship, clockdom, clockation, clockition, and clockhood.

The ogress decided to call on an old inspirationalist who had once advised her father not to worry about a giant he was worrying about. The inspirationalist had said to the ogress's father, "Don't pay any attention to it, and it will go away." And the ogress's father had paid no attention to it, and it had gone away, taking him with it, and this had pleased the ogress. The inspirationalist was now a very old man whose inspirationalism had become a jumble of mumble. "The final experience should not be mummum," he mumbled.

The ogress said, "But what is mummum?"

"Mummum," said the inspirationalist, "is what the final experience should not be." And he mumbled to a couch, lay down upon it, and fell asleep.

As the days went on, the ogre ate all the clocks in the town – mantel clocks, grandfather clocks, travelling

4–6 **clocksmith ... clockologist:** Wortschöpfungen; etwa: Uhrenschmied, Uhrwerker, Uhrenhändler, Uhriker, Uhrometrist, Uhrologe.

7 f. **clockness ... clockhood:** Wortschöpfungen; etwa: Uhrheit, Uhrismus, Uhrschaft, Uhrtum, Uhration, Uhrition, Uhrkeit.

9 **inspirationalist:** Wortschöpfung; etwa: Erleuchteter.

16 f. **jumble:** Durcheinander, Wirrwarr.

17 **mumble:** Gemurmel.

24–63,2 **mantel clock . . . steeple clock:** Kaminuhr, Standuhr, Reisewekker, Bahnhofsuhr, Wecker, Uhr mit Achttagewerk, Kirchturmuhr.

clocks, stationary clocks, alarm clocks, eight-day clocks, steeple clocks, and tower clocks – sprinkling them with watches, as if the watches were salt and pepper, until there were no more watches. People overslept, and failed to go to work, or to church, or any place else where they had to be on time. Factories closed down, shopkeepers shut up their shops, schools did not open, trains no longer ran, and people stayed at home. The town council held an emergency meeting and its members arrived at all hours, and some did not show up at all. A psychronologist was called to the witness stand to testify as to what should be done. "This would appear to be a clear case of clock-eating, but we should not jump so easily to conclusions," he said. "We have no scientific data whatever on clock-eating, and hence no controlled observation. All things, as we know, are impossible in this most impossible of all impossible worlds. That being the case, no such thing as we think has happened could have happened. Thus the situation does not fall within the frame of my discipline. Good day, gentlemen." The psychronologist glanced at where his wrist-watch should have been and, not finding it there, was disturbed. "I have less than no time at all," he said, "which means that

2 **to sprinkle:** bestreuen.
8f. **town council:** Stadtrat.
9 **emergency meeting:** Notsitzung.
11 **psychronologist:** Wortbildung aus *psychologist* und *chronologist* ›Zeitforscher‹.
witness stand: Zeugenstand.
11f. **to testify:** bestätigen, aussagen.
13f. **to jump to conclusions:** voreilige Schlüsse ziehen.
17 **this most impossible of all impossible worlds:** Anspielung auf die von dem deutschen Philosophen Gottfried Wilhelm Leibniz (1646–1716) geprägte Formel von der »besten aller möglichen Welten«.

I am late for my next appointment." And he hurriedly left the council room.

The Lord Mayor of the town, arriving late to preside over the council meeting, called a clockonomist to the stand. "What we have here," said the clockonomist, "appears on the surface to be a clockonomic crisis. It is the direct opposite of what is known, in my field, as a glut of clocks. That is, instead of there being more clocks than the consumer needs, so that the price of clocks would decrease, the consumer has consumed all the clocks. This should send up the price of clocks sharply, but we are faced with the unique fact that there are no clocks. Now, as a clockonomist, my concern is the economy of clocks, but where there are no clocks there can be no such economy. The area, in short, has disappeared."

"What do you suggest, then?" demanded the Lord Mayor.

"I suggest," said the clockonomist, "that it is now high time I go into some other line of endeavour, or transfer my clockonomy to a town which has clocks. Good day, gentlemen." And the clockonomist left the council room.

A clockosopher next took the witness chair. "If it is high time," he said, "then there is still time. The question is this: How high is high time? It means, if it means any-

3 f. **to preside over a meeting:** eine Sitzung leiten.
4/6 **clockonomist / clockonomic:** Wortbildungen aus *clock* und *economist* ›Wirtschaftswissenschaftler‹ bzw. *economic.*
7 **glut:** Überangebot, Schwemme.
19 **line of endeavour:** Interessengebiet.
20 **clockonomy:** Wortbildung aus *clock* und *economy* ›Wirtschaftswissenschaft‹.
23 **clockosopher:** Wortbildung aus *clock* und *philosopher.*

thing, which I doubt, that it is time to act. I am not an actor, gentlemen, but a clockosopher, whose osophy is based upon clocks, not necessarily upon their physical existence, but upon clocks as a concept. We still have clocks as a concept, but this meeting is concerned solely with clocks as objects. Thus its deliberations fall well outside my range of interest, and I am simply wasting time here, or would be if there were time to waste. Good day, gentlemen." And the clockosopher left the council room.

The clockmakers of the town, who had been subpoenaed, were then enjoined, in a body, from making more clocks. "You have been supplying the ogre with clocks," the Lord Mayor said severely, "whether intentionally or willy-nilly is irrelevant. You have been working hand in glove, or clock in hand, with the ogre." The clockmakers left, to look for other work.

"I should like to solve this case by deporting the ogre," the Lord Mayor said, "but, as a container of clocks, he would have to be exported, not deported. Unfortunately, the law is clear on this point: Clocks may not be exported in any save regulation containers, and the human body falls outside that legal definition."

4 **concept:** Begriff, Vorstellung, Idee.
5 **solely** (adv.): ausschließlich.
6 **deliberation:** Überlegung, Beratung.
11 f. **to subpoena:** (unter Strafandrohung) vorladen.
12 **to enjoin s.o.:** hier (jur.): jdm. ein Unterlassungsverbot erteilen.
in a body: insgesamt, zusammen, auf einmal.
14 f. **intentionally** (adv.): absichtlich.
15 **willy-nilly:** gezwungenermaßen, wohl oder übel.
16 **hand in glove:** auf vertraulichem Fuß.
18 **to deport:** verbannen, des Landes verweisen.
22 **save:** außer, ausgenommen.
regulation: vorschriftsmäßig.

Three weeks to the day after the ogre had eaten the last clock, he fell ill and took to his bed, and the ogress sent for the chief diagnostician of the Medical Academy, a diagnostician familiar with so many areas that totality itself had become to him only a part of wholeness. "The trouble is," said the chief diagnostician, "we don't know what the trouble is. Nobody has ever eaten all the clocks before, so it is impossible to tell whether the patient has clockitis, clockosis, clockoma, or clocktheria. We are also faced with the possibility that there may be no such diseases. The patient may have one of the minor clock ailments, if there are any, such as clockets, clockles, clocking cough, ticking pox, or clumps. We shall have to develop area men who will find out about such areas, if such areas exist, which, until we find out that they do, we must assume do not."

"What if he dies?" demanded the ogress eagerly.

"Then," said the chief diagnostician, "we shall bury him." And the chief diagnostician left the ogre's room and the castle.

The case of the town's clocklessness was carried to the Supreme Council, presided over by the Supreme Magistrate. "Who is prosecuting whom?" the Supreme Magistrate demanded.

3 **diagnostician:** Diagnostiker.

4 **totality:** Totalität, Gesamtheit.

9 **clockitis . . . clocktheria:** Wortschöpfungen; etwa: Uhritis, Uhrose, Uhrkom, Uhrterie.

12 **ailment:** Leiden; Unpäßlichkeit.

12f. **clockets . . . clumps:** Wortschöpfungen abgeleitet von *rickets* ›Rachitis‹, *measles* ›Masern‹, *whooping cough* ›Keuchhusten‹, *small-pox* ›Pocken‹ und *mumps* ›Mumps‹.

22 **Supreme Council:** Höchster Rat.

22f. **Supreme Magistrate:** Höchster Friedensrichter.

23 **to prosecute:** anklagen, gerichtlich verfolgen.

The Supreme Prosecutor stood up. “Let somebody say something, and I will object,” he said. “We have to start somewhere, even if we start nowhere.”

A housewife took the witness stand. “Without a clock,” she said, “I cannot even boil a three-minute egg.”

“Objection,” said the Supreme Prosecutor. “One does not *have* to boil a three-minute egg. A three-minute egg, by definition, has already been boiled for three minutes, or it wouldn’t be a three-minute egg.”

“Objection sustained,” droned the Supreme Magistrate.

The Leader of the Opposition then took the stand. “The party in power has caused the mess in the ogre’s castle,” he said.

“Objection,” said the Supreme Prosecutor. “There isn’t any party in power. The ogre was the party in power, but he no longer has any power. Furthermore, the mess caused by the party cleaning up the mess caused by the party in power, which is no longer in power, would be worse than the mess left by the party that was in power.”

“Objection sustained,” droned the Supreme Magistrate.

The Secretary of the Status Quo was the next man to take the stand. “We are not getting anywhere,” he said, “and therefore we should call a summit conference without agenda. A summit conference without agenda is destined

1 **Supreme Prosecutor:** Oberster Staatsanwalt.
6 **objection:** Einspruch.
10 **to sustain:** hier (jur.): (einem Einspruch) stattgeben.
to drone: brummen.
12 **mess:** Verwirrung, Unordnung.
23 **status quo:** Status quo, gegenwärtiger Zustand.
25 **summit conference:** Gipfelkonferenz.
26 **agenda:** Tagesordnung.

to get even less than nowhere, but its deliberations will impress those who are impressed by deliberations that get less than nowhere. This has unworked in the past, and it will unwork now. If we get less than nowhere fast enough, we shall more than hold our own, for everything is circular and cyclical, and where there are no clocks, clockwise and counterclockwise are the same."

"Objection," said the Supreme Prosecutor. "We are dealing here with a purely internal matter, caused by the consumer's having consumed all the clocks."

"Objection sustained," droned the Supreme Magistrate.

The Man in the Street now took the stand. "Why don't we use sundials?" he demanded.

"I challenge the existence of the witness," said the Supreme Prosecutor. "He says he is the Man in the Street, but he is, in fact, the Man in the Supreme Council Room. Furthermore, sundials work only when the sun is shining, and nobody cares what time it is when the sun is shining."

The Man in the Street left the witness chair, and nobody noticed his going, since the Supreme Prosecutor had established the fact that he had not been there.

There was a long silence in the Supreme Council Room, a silence so deep one could have heard a pin drop, if a pin had been dropped, but nobody dropped a pin. What

3 **to unwork:** fehlschlagen, nicht funktionieren.
5 **to hold one's own:** standhalten, seine Stellung behaupten.
6 **cyclical:** zyklisch, einen Kreislauf bildend.
7 **clockwise:** im Uhrzeigersinn.
counterclockwise: gegen den Uhrzeigersinn.
9 **internal matter:** innere Angelegenheit.
14 **sundial:** Sonnenuhr.

everybody in the Council Room heard, in the long, deep silence, was the slow tick-tock of a clock, a wall clock, the clock on the wall behind the Supreme Magistrate's bench. The officials and the witnesses and the spectators had grown so used to not hearing clocks it wasn't until the clock struck the hour that they realized there was a wall clock on the wall.

The Supreme Magistrate was the first to speak. "Unless I am mightily mistaken, and I usually am, we have here the solution to all our problems," he said, "namely, a clock. Unless there is an objection and I sustain the objection, which I do not think I shall, we will place this clock in the clock tower of the town, where it can be seen by one and all. Then we shall once again know what time it is. The situation will be cleared up, and the case dismissed."

"One minute," said the Supreme Prosecutor, and everybody waited a minute until he spoke again. "What is to prevent the ogre from eating the clock in the clock tower?"

"If you are asking me," said the Supreme Magistrate, "I do not know, but I do not have to confess my ignorance, since affirmations of this sort do not fall within my jurisdiction."

A bailiff stepped to the bench and handed the Supreme Magistrate a folded note. The Magistrate glanced at it, took off his glasses, and addressed all those present. "The ogre is dead," he announced.

"Objection," said the Supreme Prosecutor.

15 **to dismiss a case:** einen Fall als erledigt betrachten, abschließen.
22 **affirmation:** Bestätigung, Erklärung.
22 f. **jurisdiction:** Rechtsprechung; hier: Zuständigkeit.
24 **bailiff:** Gerichtsdiener.

"Objection overruled," said the Magistrate, "if you are objecting to the fact of the ogre's death."

"I accept the ogre's death as a fact," said the Prosecutor, "but we are moving too fast, and I should like to call a specialist to the stand." And he called a specialist to the stand.

"I am a collector," said the specialist. "The clock on the wall is the only clock there is. This makes it not, in fact, a clock but a collector's item, or museum piece. As such, it must be placed in the town museum. One does not spend the coins in a museum. The wineglasses in a museum do not hold wine. The suits of armour in a museum do not contain knights. The clocks in a museum do not tell time. This clock, the last clock there is, must therefore be allowed to run down, and then placed in the museum, with proper ceremonies, addresses, and the like."

"I move that this be done," the Prosecutor said.

"I should like to continue to know, as much as everybody else, what time it is," pronounced the Supreme Magistrate. "Under the circumstances, however, there is but one thing I can do in conformity with the rule which establishes the inalienable fact that the last clock is a collector's item, or museum piece. I therefore decree that the last clock, the clock here on the wall, be allowed

1 **to overrule:** hier (jur.): (einen Einspruch) ablehnen, abweisen.
9 **item:** Gegenstand.
12 **suit of armour:** Rüstung.
13 **knight:** Ritter.
15 **to run down:** ablaufen (Uhr).
17 **to move:** hier: beantragen.
19 **to pronounce:** erklären, verkünden.
21 **conformity:** Übereinstimmung.
22 **inalienable:** unveräußerlich.
23 **to decree:** entscheiden, verfügen.

to run down, and then placed in the town museum, with proper ceremonies, addresses, and the like."

The next day, at nine minutes of twelve o'clock noon, the last clock ran down and stopped. It was then placed in the town museum, as a collector's item, or museum piece, with proper ceremonies, addresses, and the like. Among those who spoke were the Lord Mayor, the Secretary of Status Quo, and the Supreme Magistrate. They all chose the same subjects, without verbs or predicates, and the subjects were these: glorious past, unlimited opportunity, challenging future, dedication, inspired leadership, enlightened followership, rededication, moral fibre, spiritual values, outer space, inner man, higher ideals, lower taxes, unflagging enthusiasm, unswerving devotion, co-ordinated efforts, dedicated rededication, and rededicated dedication.

After that, nobody in the town ever knew what time it was. Factories and schools remained closed, church bells no longer rang, because the bell ringers no longer knew when to ring them, dates and engagements were no longer made, because nobody knew when to keep them. Trains no longer ran, so nobody left town and no strangers arrived in town to tell the people what time it was. Eventually, the sands of a nearby desert moved slowly

11 **dedication:** Hingabe.
inspired: inspiriert, eingegeben.
12 **enlightened:** erleuchtet.
followership: Gefolgschaft.
rededication: erneute Hingabe.
fibre: Charakterstärke, Rückgrat.
14 **unflagging:** unermüdlich.
unswerving: unerschütterlich.
14f. **devotion:** Hingabe, Aufopferung.
24 **eventually** (adv.): schließlich, endlich.

and inexorably towards the timeless town, and in the end it was buried.

Eras, epochs, and aeons passed before a party of explorers from another planet began digging in the sands above the buried town. They were descendants of people from Earth who had reached Venus a thousand years before and intermarried with Venusians. Among them were a young man and young woman, and it was their fortune to be the first to come upon the ancient library of the old inspirationalist. Among some papers still preserved upon his desk were the last things he had written – bits of poetry from the grand Old Masters and the minor poets. One of these fragments read, "How goes the night, boy? The moomoon is down. I have not heard the clock." And the very last words his wavery pen had put on paper:

> We can make our lives sublime,
> And, departing, leave behind us,
> Mummum in the sands of time.

"What is mummum?" the young woman asked.

"I don't know," the young man said, "but something tells me we shall find a lot of it." They went on digging, and, in

1 **inexorably** (adv.): unerbittlich.
3 **era:** Ära.
aeon: Äon, Zeit-, Weltalter.
7 **to intermarry:** untereinander heiraten.
13f. **How goes ... the clock:** *Macbeth* II,1.
15 **wavery:** zittrig.
16–18 **We can make ... sands of time:** Thurber parodiert hier einen bekannten Vierzeiler aus Henry Wadsworth Longfellows (1807–82) Gedicht »Retribution«: »Lives of great men all remind us / We can make our lives sublime, / And, departing, leave behind us / Footprints on the sands of time.«
sublime: erhaben, hehr.

the end, came upon the last clock in the town museum, so clogged with sand they could not tell what it had once been used for, and so they marked it "Antique mechanism. Function uncertain. Possibly known to the ancients as mummum." And they took it back to Venus, in a cargo rocket ship, with other mysterious relics of the Time of Man on Earth.

5 **cargo:** Fracht.
6 **relic:** Überbleibsel.

Editorische Notiz

Der englische Text folgt der Ausgabe: *Vintage Thurber: A Collection, in Two Volumes, of the Best Writings and Drawings of James Thurber*, London: Hamilton, 1963, Nachdr. 1973 (Bd. 1), 1976 (Bd. 2). Das Glossar erklärt in der Regel alle Wörter, die über die Wertigkeitsstufe 4 des *Englischen Arbeitswörterbuches* von Alfred Haase (Frankfurt a. M.: Moritz Diesterweg, [7]1979) hinausgehen. Im Zweifelsfall wurde großzügig verfahren, d. h. eher eine Vokabel mehr aufgenommen als dort vorgesehen. – Die einzelnen Geschichten sind jeweils unabhängig voneinander glossiert.

Im Glossar verwendete Abkürzungen

adv.	adverb
AE	American English
arch.	archaic (veraltet)
coll.	colloquial (umgangssprachlich)
dial.	dialectal (mundartlich)
fig.	figuratively (übertragen)
frz.	französisch
jur.	jurisprudence (bei Ausdrücken aus der Rechtssprache)
o.s.	oneself
pl.	plural
poet.	poetical
s.o.	someone
s.th.	something

Verzeichnis der Werke von James Thurber

Is Sex Necessary? Or Why You Feel the Way You Do (zus. mit E. B. White), New York / London: Harper, 1929; London: Heinemann, 1930.

The Owl in the Attic and Other Perplexities, New York / London: Harper, 1931.

The Seal in the Bedroom & Other Predicaments, New York / London: Harper, 1932; London: Hamilton, 1951.

My Life and Hard Times, New York / London: Harper, 1933.

The Middle-Aged Man on the Flying Trapeze, New York / London: Harper, 1935; London: Hamilton, 1935.

Let Your Mind Alone! And Other More or Less Inspirational Pieces, New York / London: Harper, 1937; London: Hamilton, 1937.

Cream of Thurber, London: Hamilton, 1939.

The Last Flower, New York / London: Harper, 1939; London: Hamilton, 1939.

The Male Animal (zus. mit Elliot Nugent), New York: Random House, 1940; London: Hamilton, 1950.

Fables for Our Time and Famous Poems Illustrated, New York / London: Harper, 1940; London: Hamilton, 1940.

My World – and Welcome to It, New York: Harcourt, Brace, 1942; London: Hamilton, 1942.

Many Moons, New York: Harcourt, Brace, 1943; London: Hamilton, 1945.

Thurber's Men, Women, and Dogs, New York: Harcourt, Brace, 1943; London: Hamilton, 1945.

The Great Quillow, New York: Harcourt, Brace, 1944.

The Thurber Carnival, New York / London: Harper, 1945; London: Hamilton, 1945.

The White Deer, New York: Harcourt, Brace, 1945; London: Hamilton, 1946.

The Beast in Me and Other Animals, New York: Harcourt, Brace, 1948; London: Hamilton, 1949.

The 13 Clocks, New York: Simon & Schuster, 1950; London: Hamilton, 1951.

The Thurber Album, New York: Simon & Schuster, 1952; London: Hamilton, 1952.

Thurber Country, New York: Simon & Schuster, 1953; London: Hamilton, 1953.

Thurber's Dogs, New York: Simon & Schuster, 1955; London: Hamilton, 1955.

A Thurber Garland, London: Hamilton, 1955.

Further Fables for Our Time, New York: Simon & Schuster, 1956; London: Hamilton, 1956.

The Wonderful O, New York: Simon & Schuster, 1957; London: Hamilton, 1958.

Alarms and Diversions, London: Hamilton, 1957; New York: Harper, 1957.

The Years with Ross, Boston/Toronto: Atlantic Monthly / Little, Brown, 1959; London: Hamilton, 1959.

Lanterns & Lances, New York: Harper, 1961; London: Hamilton, 1961.

Credos and Curios, London: Hamilton, 1962; New York / Evanston: Harper & Row, 1962.

A Thurber Carnival, New York / Hollywood / London / Toronto: French, 1962.

Vintage Thurber, 2 Bde., London: Hamilton, 1963.

Thurber & Company, New York / Evanston / London: Harper & Row, 1966; London: Hamilton, 1967.

Selected Letters of James Thurber, hrsg. von Helen Thurber und Edward Weeks, Boston / Toronto: Little, Brown, 1981.

The Collected Letters of James Thurber, London: Hamilton, 1982.

Conversations with James Thurber, hrsg. von Thomas Fench, Jackson (Miss.) 1989.

Writings and Drawings, New York 1996.

The Thurber Letters. The Wit, Wisdom and Surprising Life of James Thurber, hrsg. von Harrison Kinney, London 2002.

Literaturhinweise

Bernstein, Burton, *Thurber: A Biography*, New York 1975.

Black, Stephen A., *James Thurber: His Masquerades*, Den Haag 1970.

Blair, Walter / Hill, Hamlin, *America's Humour: From Poor Richard to Doonesbury*, New York 1978.

Bowden, Edwin T., *James Thurber: A Bibliography*, Columbus (Ohio) 1968.

Fench, Thomas, *The Man Who Was Walter Mitty: The Life and Works of James Thurber*, The Woodlands. (Tex.) 2001.

Grauer, Neil A., *Remember Laughter. A Life of James Thurber*, Lincoln. (Neb.) 1995.

Holmes, Charles S., *The Clocks of Columbus: The Literary Career of James Thurber*. New York 1972.

– (Hrsg.), *Thurber: A Collection of Critical Essays*, Englewood Cliffs (N. J.) 1974.

Jochum, Klaus Peter: »Die Fabeln James Thurbers«, in: Peter Hambek (Hrsg.), *Die Fabel: Theorie, Geschichte und Rezeption einer Gattung*, Berlin 1982, S. 236–252.

Kenney, Catherine McGehee, *Thurber's Anatomy of Confusion*, Hamden (CT) 1984.

Kinney, Harrison, *James Thurber. His Life and Times*, New York 1997.

Morsberger, Robert E., *James Thurber*, New York 1964.

Suerbaum, Ulrich, »Thurber and Christie and Shakespeare: ›The Macbeth Murder Mystery‹«, in: *Anglistik und Englischunterricht* 23 (1984) S. 63–77.

Tobias, Richard C., *The Art of James Thurber*, Athens (Ohio) 1969.

Toombs, Sarah Eleanora, *James Thurber. An Annotated Bibliography of Criticism*, New York 1987.

Triesch, Manfred, »Men and Animals: James Thurber and the Conversion of a Literary Genre«, in: *Studies in Short Fiction* 3 (1966) S. 307–313.

Zeittafel

1894	8.12.: James Thurber in Columbus (Ohio) geboren.
1901	Verlust eines Auges bei einem Spielunfall.
1913–18	Studium an der Ohio State University, Columbus.
1918–20	Tätigkeit als »code clerk« für das State Department in Washington und Paris.
1920–24	Reporter des Columbus *Evening Dispatch*.
1922	Heirat mit Althea Adams.
1924–26	In Paris Mitarbeiter der *Chicago Tribune*.
1926	Rückkehr nach Amerika.
1927	Erste humoristische Beiträge für Harold Ross' *New Yorker*. Thurber übernimmt vorübergehend Herausgebertätigkeiten (vgl. *The Years with Ross*).
1929	*Is Sex Necessary* (mit E. B. White), Thurbers erste Buchveröffentlichung, erscheint.
1931	Geburt der Tochter Rosemary. Thurbers erste Zeichnungen erscheinen im *New Yorker*.
1933	Thurber verläßt den *New Yorker*, bleibt aber weiterhin einer der wesentlichen freien Mitarbeiter.
1935	Scheidung; zweite Ehe mit Helen Wismer.
1939	Veröffentlichung von *The Last Flower*, einer Parabel gegen den Krieg.
1940	*Fables for Our Time* und *The Male Animal*, ein Theaterstück (mit Elliot Nugent) erscheinen.
1940–41	Zahlreiche Augenoperationen, zunehmende Sehschwäche.
1946–52	Thurber opponiert offen gegen die Einschränkung der Meinungsfreiheit und die politische Hetze unter McCarthy.
1952	Fast völlig erblindet, ist Thurber gezwungen, das Zeichnen aufzugeben.
1960	*The Thurber Carnival*, eine Sammlung seiner Schriften und Zeichnungen, wird erfolgreich für die Bühne adaptiert. Thurber spielt sich selbst.
1961	Am 2. 11. stirbt James Thurber in New York.

Nachwort

I

»The power that created the poodle, the platypus, and people has an integrated sense of both comedy and tragedy«, schreibt James Thurber in einem Brief an Frances Glennon am 24. Juni 1959.[1] Thurber entscheidet sich für eine Sehweise der »reality twisted to the right into humor rather than to the left into tragedy«[2] und gilt durchaus folgerichtig auf den ersten Blick als Humorist. Er setzt ganz bewußt im oben erwähnten Brief gegen die Überbetonung des Bedeutenden und die Unterbewertung des sogenannten Humoristischen alias Trivialen die Erfahrung, »that my days, nights, and years are an unplanned combination of both elements.« Dann bezeichnet sich Thurber aber wiederum einem Kreis von Personen zugehörig, die mit dem Begriff »Humoristen« (ein irreführendes Wort für Thurber) zu benennen, die Natur ihres Dilemmas und das Dilemma ihrer Natur mißzuverstehen hieße; denn ihnen ist eigen »a genius for getting into minor difficulties: they walk into the wrong apartments, they drink furniture polish for stomach bitters, they drive their cars into the prize tulip beds of haughty neighbours, they playfully slap gangsters, mistaking them for old school friends. The little wheels of their invention are set in motion by the damp hand of melancholy.«[3] »Humour is counterbalance.«[4]

James Thurber ist am ehesten als Kombination gegensätzlicher Elemente zu begreifen. Eine möglicherweise tragische Situation erhält durch triviale Vertracktheiten eine Wendung ins Komische, eine an sich bedeutungslose Einzelheit wie Mr Bruhls Narbe im Gesicht wird zum Ausgangspunkt bedeuten-

1 Zit. nach: Helen Thurber / Edward Weeks (Hrsg.), *Selected Letters of James Thurber*, Harmondsworth 1982.

2 Peter A. Scholl, »James Thurber«, in: *Dictionary of Literary Biography*, Bd. 11, S. 512 [im folgenden zit. als: DLB].

3 James Thurber, »Preface to a Life (My Life and Hard Times)«, in: J. T., *The Thurber Carnival*, Harmondsworth 1984, S. 208.

4 Brief an Francis Glennon vom 24. Juni 1959.

der Entwicklungen. Der Melancholiker schafft sich das Gegengewicht des Humors, hinter dem sich gleichermaßen, wie man noch sehen wird, ein Moralist verbirgt. Thurber wurde der großstädtische »upper middle-class Easterner« und blieb doch »an Ohio boy at heart«, »a self-exiled Midwesterner« auf der Suche nach dem »Great Good Place, which he conceives to be an old Colonial house, surrounded by elms and maples«[5], der doch das hektische Leben einer Generation führt, von der er sagt: »We knew where we were, all right, but we wouldn't go home. Ours was the generation that stayed up all night. Indeed, we spent so little time in bed most of us had only one child.«[6]

II

James Thurber begann seine journalistische, schriftstellerische Tätigkeit 1920 als Mitarbeiter verschiedener Zeitungen in seiner Heimatstadt Columbus (Ohio). 1925 lebte er in Frankreich und betreute die Pariser Ausgabe der *Chicago Tribune*. 1926 zog er nach New York und wurde Reporter bei der *New York Evening Post*, 1927 dann ziemlich regelmäßiger Mitarbeiter bei der berühmten Zeitschrift *The New Yorker*, wobei er viel zur Entwicklung ihres spezifischen Tones beitrug, wie er heute noch von gegenwärtigen Starschreibern des Blattes, z. B. Donald Barthelme und Woody Allen, gepflegt wird. Die Wertschätzung, die Thurber auch als Zeichner genoß, wird aus einer Bemerkung von Henri Matisse ersichtlich. Als dieser einmal nach New York gekommen war, antwortete er auf die Frage eines Reporters, wen er für den besten Zeichner in den USA hielte: »Der einzige gute Zeichner, den ihr in New York habt, ist ein Mann namens Thurber.«[7] Ein Urteil, dem sich auch George Grosz anschloß.

Über Thurbers Arbeitsweise wird folgende Geschichte kolportiert: Seine Frau Althea habe ihn überzeugt, daß er zu lange über seinen Manuskripten brüte. Statt dessen solle er sich

5 DLB, S. 507.

6 Brief an Frances Glennon vom 24. Juni 1959.

7 Zit. nach: Gert Haffmans (Hrsg.), *Der Rabe*, Nr. 2, Zürich 1983, S. 84 f.

lieber einen Wecker hinstellen und absenden, was immer er innerhalb von fünfundvierzig Minuten fertig bringe. Diese Methode entpuppte sich als erfolgreich,[8] und daraus erklären sich wohl auch einige formale Strukturen von Thurbers »Pieces« (wie er sie selbst nannte).

Die Vielfalt und Widersprüchlichkeit, die Mehrschichtigkeit der modernen Welt, das Chaotische und Ungeordnete der ihn umgebenden Realität und auch der eigenen Person mit ihren »oddities« und bizarren Begebenheiten ließen sich kaum durch einen wohlgestalteten, auf Kausalität beruhenden *plot* erfassen. Grundlegend ist vielmehr das vereinzelt Anekdotische, die »narrative anecdote«, mit der Möglichkeit der pointierten Zuspitzung und dem blitzartigen Verweis auf weitere Zusammenhänge. Die Erzählung wird durch einen Einfall oder eine Begebenheit von einem Punkt aus in Gang gesetzt und schreitet in den geschlosseneren Erzählungen von diesem Punkt aus, in mehreren Stationen sich entfaltend, weiter fort (z. B. in *The Remarkable Case of Mr Bruhl* und *The Private Life of Mr Bidwell*), oder es werden Phänomene, auch Slapstick-Elemente addiert, Anekdoten aneinandergereiht (z. B. in *A Sequence of Servants*), oder der Grundeinfall wird durch Aufhäufen weiterer Episoden oder Übersteigerung nach dem Schneeballprinzip in eine Überdrehungsgeschichte entwickelt (z. B. in *The Night The Ghost Got In* oder *More Alarms At Night*).

In *The Macbeth Murder Mystery* (einer Art »anecdotal essay«) ist die zufällige Begegnung mit einer Frau, die versehentlich statt des gewünschten Kriminalromans eine Shakespeare-Tragödie erworben und diese mit der Erwartungshaltung an einen Kriminalroman gelesen hatte, Ausgangspunkt einer vor diesem Hintergrund folgerichtigen, sich weiterspinnenden neuen Lesart, die die Tragödie in einen Kriminalroman verwandelt. – Die Erzählung *The Night the Dam Broke* wird in Gang gesetzt von der fälschlichen Behauptung, daß ein Staudamm gebrochen sei und die Stadt zu überschwemmen drohe. Diese Nachricht verbreitet sich wie ein Lauffeuer und führt, von Thurber immer weiter überdreht mit allerlei slapstickhaften Begeben-

8 Vgl. DLB, S. 509.

heiten, zur Massenpanik; die Bewohner fliehen aus der Stadt, bis sich herausstellt, daß es blinder Alarm war.
Verwundert scheint Thurber die Verrücktheit der Realität zur Kenntnis zu nehmen; vor den Phänomenen stehend läßt er sich durch Bizzarerien jedoch nicht verwirren, vielmehr zeigt sich hier sein »verrückter Genius«, dessen Formel lautet: »Thurber hat die Konfusion unter feste Kontrolle gebracht.«[9] Er selbst war der Meinung: »The undisciplined mind [. . .] is far better adapted to the confused world in which we live today than the streamlined mind.«[10] War es also wirklich der auf fünfundvierzig Minuten eingestellte Wecker, der ihn die Konfusion unter Kontrolle bringen ließ?

III

Als Sechsjähriger verliert James Thurber bei einem Spielunfall sein linkes Auge. Einer seiner Brüder hatte ihm versehentlich einen Pfeil ins Auge geschossen. Seit den vierziger Jahren nimmt nach mehreren erfolglosen Operationen auch die Sehschwäche des intakten Auges zu. Sieht er von daher nicht schon zwangsläufig die Wirklichkeit durch eine andere Brille? – Mit seiner Fähigkeit zur Selbstironie reflektiert Thurber in einem Brief: »In every other way I am fine. I am very happy, when not driving at night, and my wife is very happy too, when not being driven by me at night.«[11]
In *The Macbeth Murder Mystery* wird Shakespeare durch die vermeintlich falsche Brille des Kriminalromans betrachtet. Der Witz ergibt sich aus dem Aufeinanderprallen und Austauschen von an sich feststehenden Lesarten, wodurch die festgefügten Wert- und Gattungsvorstellungen von Detektivroman und Tragödie, von trivialer und hoher Literatur durcheinander gebracht werden und ins Wanken geraten. Der Dialog, das Frage- und Antwortspiel gibt den Argumentationsverlauf eines

9 Zit. nach: Robert von Berg (Hrsg.); »Ein erlesener Jahrgang«, in: *Süddeutsche Zeitung*, 11./12. Mai 1985.
10 DLB, S. 513.
11 Brief an Herman and Dorothy Miller vom August 1935.

literaturkritischen Essays wieder; die Verwirrung der Lesarten ist Grundlage der Geschichte und wird zugunsten einer neuen Lesart und Sehweise unter Kontrolle gebracht.

Als »interpreter of modern life« schreibt Thurber gegen die Regeln an, die festlegen wollen, wann welche Brille wofür aufzusetzen, wann welche Sehweise die vermeintlich angemessene ist. Thurber steht für »freedom, independence, the irrepressible stuff of life which refuses to be caught in formulas and conventions.«[12]

In diesem Sinne wendet er sich gleichermaßen gegen Leute, »die eine Illusion nicht von einer anderen unterscheiden können.« Er berichtet »von einer Nonne aus dem Mittelalter, die ihre Netzhautstörungen mit Gottesvisionen verwechselte, obgleich sie nur ein Zehntel der heiligen Symbole sah, die ich wahrnehme.«[13]

Aus solcherart Visionen ist dann der Stoff von *The Admiral on the Wheel*, worin auch über die Befreiung reflektiert wird, die sich aus einer verschobenen – brillenlosen – Wahrnehmung der Wirklichkeit ergibt, einer Wahrnehmungsweise, die uns nicht mehr nur zum »prisoner of reality« macht.

Mit der anekdotischen Erinnerung *Draft Board Nights* gelingt Thurber eine Schwejkiade, in der er nicht allein die verschobene Wahrnehmung von Realität thematisiert, sondern worin real zugewiesene Rollen einfach vertauscht werden. Den Hintergrund bildet die eigentlich groteske Situation, daß der Erzähler insgesamt zehn Mal zur Musterung gerufen wird, jedes Mal jedoch wegen seiner schlechten Augen vom Militär zurückgestellt wird. Er greift schließlich selbst zum Stethoskop, und plötzlich gilt er selbst als Musterungsarzt, ohne daß irgend jemandem Unstimmigkeiten auffielen. Zum Schluß bleibt aber auch der Erzähler nicht verschont davon, weitere Male zur Musterung gerufen zu werden, ohne daß er nunmehr irgend jemandem als vermeintlicher, ehemaliger ›Musterungsarzt‹ bekannt gewesen wäre. So wird das Militär in seiner Ignoranz als Institution desavouiert.

12 Charles S. Holmes, *The Clocks of Columbus. The Literary Career of James Thurber*, New York 1972, S. 158.

13 Beide Zitate aus dem Brief an Dr. Gordon Bruce vom 9. Dezember 1948.

IV

Mit *The Private Life of Mr Bidwell* und *The Remarkable Case of Mr Bruhl* liegen wohl zwei der dichtesten Geschichten von Thurber vor. Beide, Mr Bidwell und Mr Bruhl, verlieren ihre Identität. Während Mr Bruhl seine tatsächliche Identität nicht mehr aufrechterhalten kann und der Obsession erliegt, aufgrund einer Narbe im Gesicht eine fiktive Identität annehmen zu müssen, stiehlt sich Mr Bidwell aus seinem Leben heraus, indem er sein ureigenstes, privates Leben auf einige fixe Ideen reduziert. Seine Identität gründet sich nur noch auf den jeweils aktuellen Tick, hinter dem er verschwindet. Mr Bruhl verschwindet, weil er die fiktive Identität, jemand anderer, ein Verbrecher erster Klasse, zu sein, genauso akzeptiert, wie andere es für gegeben nehmen und ihn erschießen.
Beiden ist die Ausgangslage gemein, ein unspektakuläres, langweiliges, in Konventionen verhaftetes Leben zu führen. Aus dieser Normalität beziehen sie ihre Identität, wogegen beide auf ihre Art rebellieren. Thurber zeigt, welche Gefahren erwachsen, wenn man sich aus Vorgegebenheiten löst, aggressiv und doch daneben zielend wie Mr Bruhl oder eher regressiv und an sich selbst vorbei wie Mr Bidwell. Identität geht auf jeden Fall verloren, statt dessen werden Obsessionen bestimmend. Eine Gefahr wird damit Gegenstand von Erzählungen, die sicherlich auch für Thurber selbst vorausgesetzt werden muß; für jemanden nämlich, der sich nicht zufrieden gibt mit den scheinbar festgefügten Realitätsformeln und für Vorstellungskraft, Verwirrung und konstruktive Konfusion eintritt. Zum anderen ist hierin aber auch eine Kritik Thurbers an den von ihm beschriebenen Gegebenheiten moderner Zivilisation zu sehen. Die herkömmliche Ordnung und Übereinkunft unterdrückt das Irrationale und die Ängste, die freilich, wenn sie einmal Platz greifen, auf die gewohnte Ordnung zerstörerisch wirken. – Sichtbar wird dieser Zusammenhang in der Figur von Mr Bidwell, der noch bei seinen Rückzugsgefechten, in seinen fixen Ideen die Realität widerspiegelt, gegen die er doch eigentlich rebelliert. Er verfällt auf nichts Besseres als auf das Multiplizieren von Zahlen

und das Zählen von Schritten, worin der Nachhall einer Ordnung zu sehen ist, die allein das Zählbare und Abgezirkelte, das sogenannte Nützliche gelten läßt. Hätte Mr Bidwell, statt unterdrückend seinen Atem für abzählbare Sekunden anzuhalten, nicht doch besser losprusten sollen?

V

Am deutlichsten wird der zivilisationskritische Aspekt in Thurbers Fabeln. 1940 erschien mit *Fables for Our Time* die erste Sammlung, 1956 gefolgt von *Further Fables for Our Time*. Hinter dem Humoristen wird der Moralist und Satiriker sichtbar, der seinen Humor gezielt als Gegengewicht einsetzt.
Die Fabel wird im allgemeinen beschrieben als »kurze episch-didaktische Gattung der Tierdichtung [. . .], die eine allgemein anerkannte Wahrheit, einen moralischen Satz, eine praktische Lebensweisheit an Hand eines überraschenden, doch analogen Beispiels in uneigentlicher Darstellung veranschaulicht und besonders aus der Übertragung menschlicher Verhältnisse, Sitten, auch der Rede, auf die beseelte oder unbeseelte Natur [. . .] witzig-satirische oder moralisch-belehrende Effekte erzielt.«[14] Typisch besonders für die Tierfabel ist die Benutzung von feststehenden, den Tieren zugeschriebenen Charaktereigenschaften, wodurch sich eine eigene Charakterschilderung erübrigt. – In der Literatur des 20. Jahrhunderts ist die Fabel eine nicht sehr häufig benutzte Form, dennoch gibt es einige hervorragende Beispiele bei Franz Kafka und Robert Musil.
Thurber will nicht die vorgegebene Form der Fabel erfüllen, sondern die Form wird benutzt und den eigenen Zwecken angeglichen. Er arbeitet nicht mit feststehenden, Tieren zugeschriebenen Eigenschaften und beschränkt sich überdies nicht auf Tiere als Darstellungsmittel, sondern bezieht Uhren, Menschenfresser, Außerirdische und den Menschen selbst mit ein. Die Darstellung ist dabei immer uneigentlich, bis hin zum Parabelhaften in *The Last Clock*. Die Tiergestalten sind eher

14 Gero von Wilpert, *Sachwörterbuch der Literatur*, Stuttgart [6]1979, S. 258.

Figurationen von menschlichen Typen, Charakteren, auch von gesellschaftlich bedingten Sachverhalten. Die zentrale Gestalt in *The Wolf Who Went Places* ist der ewig Leichtsinnige, der Prahler, der Rekordsüchtige, der noch nicht einmal etwas wie ein Restrisiko kennt. In dieser Fabel könnte man natürlich ein stark lehrhaftes Element erblicken, denn das Verhalten des Wolfes wird als ein abschreckendes, schlechtes Beispiel vorgeführt: »[. . .] the hellbent get where they are going« (S. 51). Zumindest ist hierin (wie auch in *The Human Being and the Dinosaur*) ein Appell an die Vernunft erkennbar. Im Gegensatz zu älteren Fabelformen wird jedoch keine gängige Moral, keine allgemein anerkannte Wahrheit transportiert. Thurbers Fabeln korrigieren das Klischee der Gattung, die sie selbst repräsentieren. In *The Peacelike Mongoose* etwa prangert er satirisch, fast grotesk zugespitzt gerade die Moral der Moral an: »[. . .] if the enemy doesn't get you, your own folks may« (S. 48). Verweigerungshaltungen erlauben die vermeintlich vernünftigen, sich allein auf Macht gründenden, auf Mitmachen gerichteten Anforderungen der Gesellschaft an den einzelnen nicht.

Ein etwas pessimistischerer Grundton in Thurbers späteren Jahren ist kaum zu überhören. Doch steht er für eine Haltung, die in der Aufforderung zusammengefaßt ist: »[. . .] let us not look back in anger, or forward in fear, but around in awareness.«[15]

Werner Gotzmann

15 DLB, S. 525.

“I suppose all that you men think about is war.”

Inhalt